TRUE RADIANCE

True Radiance

FINDING GRACE
IN THE
SECOND HALF OF LIFE

Lisa Mladinich

servant
AN IMPRINT OF
FRANCISCAN MEDIA
Cincinnati, Ohio

Cover design by Mary Ann Smith
Cover image © Getty Images | Ralf Nau
Book design by Mark Sullivan

LIBRARY OF CONGRESS CATALOGING-IN-PUBLICATION DATA
Mladinich, Lisa.
True radiance : finding grace in the second half of life / Lisa Mladinich.
pages cm
Includes bibliographical references and index.
ISBN 978-1-61636-907-1 (alk. paper)
1. Catholic women—Religious life. 2. Middle-aged women—Religious life. 3. Aging—Religious aspects—Christianity. I. Title.
BX2353.M65 2015
248.8'43—dc23
2015027622

ISBN 978-1-61636-907-1

Published by Servant Books, an imprint of Franciscan Media
28 W. Liberty St.
Cincinnati, OH 45202
www.FranciscanMedia.org

Printed in the United States of America.
Printed on acid-free paper.
15 16 17 18 19 5 4 3 2 1

To the most beautiful women I have ever known:

To the Blessed Mother, Mary, Ever Virgin, for the perfection of your love for your spiritual children; for your protection, guidance, and intercession. I love you, and I thank you for leading me back to your divine Son, Jesus.

To my daughter, on the verge of womanhood. Theresa, my darling girl, I pray that you will always know your worth as a daughter of God. Your sweetness and beauty are daily glimpses of heaven for me. Your arrival was the beginning of the very best years of my life.

To my wise and gentle mother, Barbara Kirkwood; my adorable mother-in-law, Margot Mladinich; my brilliant and funny best friend, Annette Scarpa; my inspiring, faith-filled sisters: Christine Rathier, Nancy Baum, and Elizabeth Selden; and my very special cousins, Marianne DiCorpo and Debra Silvia —thank you! You have been there for me, countless times, with your love and feminine wisdom. You are all very beautiful.

In tender remembrance of my exquisite grandmother, Irene Kirkwood; my beautiful godmother, Yvonne Crompton; and my gorgeous aunts, Nancy Donndelinger and Jeanne Lewis—I miss you all so much! May your souls eternally enjoy the peace and infinite beauty of heaven.

Contents

••

So many special people helped in the creation of this book.

First, I'd like to thank my family for their loving support. Charlie and Theresa, I would be lost without you. The love that God brings to fruition in our family life is the river that runs through everything I do. Your fingerprints and heart prints are all over my life and woven into the pages of this book.

To my editors, Claudia Volkman and Louise Paré: Your intelligence, warmth, and encouragement have blessed me greatly. You are magnificent, beautiful women. I am very proud to know you and grateful for your wisdom and generosity. I'm so happy we met and I am grateful to Donna-Marie Cooper O'Boyle for introducing us!

To Pat Gohn, my beautiful friend, mentor, cheerleader, and prayer partner: You have inspired and encouraged me all the way through this project, and I simply cannot thank you enough. Your influence has made me a better writer and a happier human being. You are precious to me, and I count myself very blessed to be your friend. May God continue to bless your life and your ministry to women.

To Annette Scarpa, Elizabeth Christie, and so many beautiful friends in the Immaculate Heart of Mary homeschool network: Thank you for going out of your way to lighten my load while I was writing, working, and homeschooling. Your prayers and acts of kindness saved my sanity. I can never hope to repay you, but I will always be grateful. God bless you!

To everyone who contributed their insights and stories to my research: I wish I could throw a big party and bring you together, from all across the country! I'd love to give you the gift that each of you gave me: to share in each other's radiance and celebrate the work that has been so blessed by your kindness.

In alphabetical order, I salute you: Lori Bartels, Tracey Bellucci, Bernadette Brandon, Jennifer Caiazzo, Sarah Christmyer, Erin Brown Conroy, Kay Cruise, Theresa Doyle-Nelson, Karina Fabian, Maggie Geene, Dr. Jane Gilroy, Lisa Goddard, Nina Hardy, Kimberly Hartman, Lisa Hendey, Marie Hosdil, Ellen Gable Hrkach, Helen Jones, Shelly Henley Kelly, Barbara Kirkwood, Sister Janina "Bernarda" Krajewska, Dr. Peter Kreeft, Margot Mladinich, Suzanne Moran, Dr. Ann Nolte, Louise Paré, Mary Lou Rosien, Elizabeth Schmeidler, Elizabeth Selden, Dr. Jem Sullivan, Susan Tassone, Vicki Thorn, Erin von Uffel, Juliet Way, Winnie Weir, Clare Westlund, and Jane Wigutow. Thank you all, from the heart!

Finally, to the many women and men with whom it is my pleasure to be connected on social media: In your friendship, I have found a rich and edifying source of spiritual support in my life and in my work. Thank you for your prayers and words of encouragement. You are Church to me, in a special way, and you remain in my daily prayers.

"Magic mirror in my hand, who is the fairest in the land?"[1]

The evil queen's well-known question in the story of *Snow White* still holds relevance for many of us. The mirror knows all, sees all, tells all. Or so we assume. In her fear that her beauty was waning, the queen could not tolerate a younger, prettier, and more virtuous rival in her kingdom. Her vanity tells her that she doesn't have to, either.

We may believe that there are no such things as magic mirrors anymore, yet many of us still behave as if they exist. And we consult them frequently.

The magic mirror in the old fairy tale has morphed into a modern cultural wizard that we visit every day. Magic mirrors are the ubiquitous smartphones we carry in our pockets or purses directing our gaze to websites and social media feeds. They are computers or tablets that, with a single click, are ready to shower us with all the news or trends that showcase our latest defects or imperfections. Magic mirrors come with remote controls and glow with 800 cable channels, and print versions line our coffee tables and bookshelves. Hair and nail salons and shopping malls offer magic-kingdom-like solutions to the ways we are duped by the magic mirror's faulty standards of beauty and value.

What has the magic mirror been saying to you lately? What do you see? More important, what do you believe? Whose opinion counts ultimately? And, what truth might we discern? How can we find God's wisdom among the many messages we see and hear?

For those of us facing midlife and beyond, we find a faith-filled confidant in the person of Lisa Mladinich, author of *True Radiance: Finding Grace in the Second Half of Life.*

Lisa Mladinich is well acquainted with the power of the magic mirror and its ill-fitting reflection of beauty. A former actress turned Catholic catechist and author, today Mladinich holds up the mirror to our faith in Christ and illumines the dignity and purpose we possess as women made in the image of God. That simple truth shines brightly in every chapter of this bold little book.

I'm reminded of the great apostle, St. Paul, who penned, "When I was a child, I spoke like a child, I thought like a child, I reasoned like a child" (1 Corinthians 13:11). How important to approach our days with a holy maturity whereby we give up childish ways—without sacrificing our joy and innocence as children of God—knowing that we are that much closer to the day when we will meet Our Lord. Indeed, St. Paul continued, "For now we see in a mirror dimly, but then face to face. Now I know in part; then I shall understand fully, even as I have been fully understood" (1 Corinthians 13:12).

True Radiance takes aim at some of the falsehoods that mar and malign our feminine genius. Besides her own encounters with the healing love of God, Lisa Mladinich's personal research and discussions with other women in the second half of life offer perspective and encouragement from the front lines of post-menopausal living.

Mladinich's anecdotes and her confident faith challenge us to lovingly reconsider the things that distract us from understanding true beauty. She writes, "Like anything that isn't God himself, the quest for physical beauty can consume too much of our time, money, and attention—when, in the second half of our lives, quite frankly, we've got better things to do."

We *do* have better things to do! For me, I love reading books that tell honest stories. I appreciate that Lisa Mladinich writes in a way that honors my faith *and* my intellect. She's an all-in Catholic. Her awe and zeal for the faith is refreshingly invigorating. Yet she manages to tickle my funny bone while offering a reverential look at this blessed and, at times, bewildering phase of life.

Is it possible to find God speaking to you through a hot flash? Or truth as you battle with a bout of brain fog? Can you sense a smile from heaven in your dog's antics? Or find peace in a sentence from the *Catechism*? Lisa Mladinich's book offers that and more.

Proverbs 31:30 reveals that "a woman who fears the Lord is to be praised." Faith and true beauty go hand in hand. And often we women learn this best from the examples of other women. From her touching reversion story describing the Blessed Mother leading her closer to Jesus to her chapter on the need for friendships with saints and other women, Lisa Mladinich never forgets that it is grace that fuels a heart's movement toward God and others. Along with the women she profiles in this book, she offers authentic ways to uncover grace in our own experiences as we mature.

I first met Lisa Mladinich in 2010 after reading her compelling account of her journey back to the Catholic faith. I interviewed her for my podcast, *Among Women*, and we stayed in touch after that. Since then, I've come to appreciate Lisa's leadership and creative spark as we've worked collaboratively within the community that is the Catholic Writers Guild, and within the online catechetical initiative that she founded, Amazing Catechists. I've enjoyed her columns in *Catechist* magazine and her previous books, *Be an Amazing Catechist: Inspire the Faith of Children*, and *Be an Amazing Catechist: Sacramental Preparation*.

Gifted in working with both children and adults, Lisa is an evangelist for what it true and good and beautiful. Her heart for women comes to the fore in *True Radiance: Finding Grace in the Second Half of Life*. Her book's subtitle aptly describes her *modus operandi*...she knows where to find grace. What Lisa Mladinich learns never sits idle or grows cold—she always shares it, giving it away with grace and humility.

This book holds no glum resignation or a like-it-or-lump-it attitude. Rather, it's a full-blown gratitude guide for the kind of renewal and renaissance that can only flow from a faith that, as Augustine wrote, is ever ancient yet ever new. It's a look at becoming beauty. More than skin-deep, true beauty properly points to sanctity—and ultimately to heaven.

One of my favorite phrases from the *Compendium of Social Doctrine of the Church* is "something of the glory of God shines on the face of every person."[2]

Memorize this: Something of the glory of God shines on your face. Then remind yourself the next time you come face-to-face with a mirror.

The human person who fully lives her dignity gives glory to God. Let *True Radiance* help you reflect on that truth.

—Pat Gohn, author of *Blessed, Beautiful, and Bodacious: Celebrating the Gift of Catholic Womanhood*

True Radiance

For she is more beautiful than the sun,
and excels every constellation of the stars.

—Wisdom 7:29

Any discussion of authentic beauty is intensely interesting to women. Invariably, the women I interview brighten at the mention of a true, interior beauty that increases throughout their lives. They instinctively recognize the truth of this beguiling notion because their own interior radiance confirms it.

We think about beauty more than we realize: throughout the day, in relation to ourselves and others, as well as in our surroundings. We are hardwired to appreciate all that is innocent, alluring, elegant, or graceful. Perhaps this hardwiring is the reason it hurts so much that our culture-shaping media averts its influential gaze from our aging faces and bodies—just as we're maturing spiritually and getting some soul-invigorating traction with the Christian call to love.

Long ago, I interviewed a favorite Catholic author and philosopher, Dr. Peter Kreeft, and asked him who his role models were. "Christ, of course," he replied, immediately. "He is the role model par excellence. And Mother Teresa; she is my idea of a supermodel." We laughed about his use of the term, since "supermodel" implies a statuesque young girl with full lips and wide-set eyes, her thin figure a blank canvas upon which designers may drape and stretch their creations at will—with never a lump or crease in sight.

Mother Teresa, on the other hand—tiny to start and bent even smaller from years of service, wrinkled and creased over every inch of her face and hands, her teeth cheerily crooked, her close-set eyes radiating both joy and sorrow at once—would never pass muster with the fashionable crowd. Even in middle age she looked too old, too small, too rough to be called beautiful. But the world, with its slickly packaged ideals of beauty, can never hope to compare with the radiance of a soul so attractive that attendees at her public appearances sometimes burst into tears when Mother Teresa left a room.

It is a wake-up call to our notions of beauty that our beloved Lord Jesus is hidden beneath the appearance of bread and wine in the Eucharist. So easily overlooked or even despised, his sacramental presence is a silent one, so meek and reserved that even the devout may struggle to grasp its significance. As the incomparable model for human perfection, Christ shows us the depths of humility required for his holy wisdom to take root in our hearts—and with this wisdom, true beauty and true radiance of spirit.

But it's easy to fall into confusion. The world peddles falsehood and despair because it is profitable to do so, creating an image for our comparison that can never be achieved in life. We know this. We abhor it. We rail against it. And yet we crave what the world sells, victims of a con so effective that, even knowing the girlish supermodel is lit, painted, and airbrushed into glowing artifice, we resent her for succeeding where we have failed.

Yet, as prayerful women age physically, we can become ageless in the spiritual life. Many of us experience the agreeable paradox of a faith grown mature enough to be childlike, one that relies on God's plan more than our own. Our mental faculties may indeed be less nimble, but we may also be gifted with a tender forgetfulness that makes peace with the past. As we move into the second half of our lives, we become more oriented toward serving others as an expression of our love for God; and in that shift of focus, we become more beautiful than we have ever been.

Even though we still want to be attractive—and most women agree that it is important to take proper care of ourselves—we sense a turning point, a crossroads at which our unspoken feminine priorities are shifting. I believe this is a singular moment in a woman's life, an opportunity to go deeper into humility and an awareness of the divine in the ordinary moments of our lives. Likewise, it is a chance to see our conversation with God in a new way, expressed in the natural cycles of our spiritual and physical evolution as Christian women. It is a chance to find our most beautiful selves in a way more real than we have ever experienced before.

This book is an attempt to invite you in out of the cold of our youth-obsessed culture. As you already know, our crassly commercial media craves your money, not your happiness, so degrading your self-image is a shortcut to getting its hands on your "beauty dollars." Mind you, I use creams and hair goop and a modicum of makeup, quite enjoying the lift they give me. But like anything that isn't God himself, the quest for physical beauty can consume too much of our time, money, and attention—when, in the second half of our lives, quite frankly, we've got better things to do.

Whatever your vocation or state of health, your marital status or economic class, it is my privilege to be writing for you, my precious sister in Christ. You are loved by your Creator in an intimate and personal way. He abides in your inmost being, where you are most purely yourself, and he speaks through the delicate human loveliness of the body that has become such a part of your identity.

True feminine beauty, designed by God to give a foretaste of heaven to humanity, is a concept that has been stolen from us. It has been warped into an endless commercial for a false and superficial standard no woman can ever achieve. I, for one, object.

So let's steal it back.

Chapter One

MIRROR, MIRROR:
Finding Strength in Our Interior Beauty

Charm is deceitful and beauty is vain,
    but a woman who fears the Lord is to be praised.

—Proverbs 31:30

I'm not a saint or a mystic, but I had a striking encounter with God not long ago that altered the way I see myself, both as a woman and as a child of God. In one sudden and luminous moment, everything inside me shifted so that I could live with more freedom and more joy. And do you want to know something funny? It all started with a pair of pajamas.

My Breakthrough Moment

One spring evening in 2014, I was settling in for the night at a hotel outside of St. Louis, Missouri. Flown in by my publisher to give some workshops for catechists the next day, I was reading over my presentation notes, which were a rumpled mess like me, after a long day of travel. I'd already brushed my teeth and slipped into pajamas that are great for air travel because they weigh next to nothing and take up very little space in my carry-on bag. They're also somewhat clingy, which makes them pretty unflattering, since they hide very little. Every time I wear them, I dream of getting in better shape and looking like the young, digitally-enhanced model on the original packaging. (Weren't these pajamas supposed to make me look like *her*?)

I was overtired from the stress of getting my house and family in New York squared away before I left, the last-minute craziness of preparing my talks, and a hectic day of schedules and connecting flights. Running parallel and close to the hotel bed was a large closet with mirrored doors in which, bathed in the bright glow of a large side-table lamp, I could see my image very clearly. There was nothing in my reflection that I hadn't already noted and catalogued in detail over the previous weeks leading up to my trip, so it shouldn't have shocked me the way it did.

However, the declining state of my appearance had recently been a source of irritation—ironically while I was intensively interviewing women for this book on authentic beauty. We talked over the many ways the best qualities of prayerful women are enhanced as they age, and I was coming to the conclusion that the second half of life is our best time of all. Yet, from the way my skin had lost its elasticity around my eyes and chin to those annoying extra pounds rolling around my middle, the sagging, middle-aged woman reflected in the hotel mirror brought me up short—and I started to cry.

It's over, I thought. *I'm not young anymore. I look awful, and it's only going to get worse.*

Because a well of grief had been rising for many days, the tears were a gushing relief, and as I prayed and yielded this flood of emotion to God, I sensed him drawing near. In the intimate and surprising way that he sometimes communicates, he showed me something I hadn't understood before. As I gazed into my own eyes in the mirror, vivid and inviting images filled my mind. I saw the most important relationships in my life for what they have become—through daily acts of love, prayer and sacrifice, sacramental life, and the extraordinary mercy of God. Through a sort of interior vision, I saw how my family life had been flooded with grace and healing: the sweetness of our words to one another, the many small acts of kindness and forgiveness that make our life together immeasurably precious.

Against the stark background of my past, this interior vision was like arriving without warning in a cool, sunlit clearing after a long, hot climb up a rugged, but beautiful, mountain. Traumatic experiences as a young woman had ensured that my early married life was burdened with unresolved pain that stressed my home life almost to the breaking point. Finally, depressed and hopeless, I tumbled headlong into conversion at the age of thirty-three, through a newfound friendship with the Blessed Virgin Mary. My life began to bloom as I learned to cling to sacramental life and to the person of Jesus Christ. Many years and countless healings later, I found myself in that hotel room in St. Louis, feeling reborn once again.

The experience of looking into my own eyes and seeing what God saw in me was brief, but suffused with grace. He showed me that I was, at that moment, the most loving person I had ever been and that he was pleased with me. He didn't remind me of my habitual sins or show me the horrendous failures of my past. He highlighted the changes in me and showered me with an affection that was profoundly reassuring. So in the glow from the lamplight, I no longer saw an aging woman whose looks were crumbling to dust; I saw a woman growing in beauty, even *becoming* beauty.

A profound peace swept over me, and I felt drenched in gratitude and love. What had seemed like a monstrous pile of work scattered across the hotel bedspread suddenly coalesced into the simple talking points I needed for the next day, and I easily dispatched the remaining tasks before turning out the lights. My thoughts were luminous and childlike, filled with delight at a newfound sense of trust. I woke the next day brimming with enthusiasm, and I presented both workshops in a liberated, natural spirit of love and confidence that surpassed every other experience I had ever had, either as a presenter in recent years or as an actress, long ago. I love public speaking, but this was the most fun with it that I'd ever had.

The Gift

It was surely no coincidence that the previous Christmas I asked God for just one gift: the grace of a *radical* trust in him. I love the stories of saints and biblical heroes. Their courage inspires me to take risks and live with more passion. It is both tragic and thrilling to know that Christians in our own times, in the Middle East and other parts of the world, have accepted martyrdom rather than deny their love for Jesus Christ. Even young children have stood firm in the face of the cruelest and most violent threats, giving their lives rather than wavering in their commitment. Heroism of that magnitude simply does not happen without a radical, ironclad trust in God.

I long to be what St. Hildegard of Bingen called "a feather on the breath of God," a soul completely yielded to his perfect will.[3] Ever since my pajama-clad encounter with God, this new-and-improved sense of trust has been a great grace and an answered prayer. I am far from being in a perfect state of confidence and communion with God, but lately, when I encounter obstacles and challenges, I remember the night in that Missouri hotel and try to think of jumping into God's arms and *expecting* him to catch me.

God keeps reassuring me that I am not alone, that he hears my cries for help, and that he makes my little efforts to trust him bear beautiful fruit. He tells me that my value as his daughter and as a woman is increasing, not fading away.

Interior Beauty Is Real Beauty

As our interior lives deepen over time, so does our feminine beauty. As we become more receptive and more docile to the will of God, our feminine nature blossoms and finds fulfillment in ways that a life lived selfishly never can. In many ways, this emptying of self is the greatest adventure of all, for in it, we make room within our hearts for Jesus Christ, the Lord of Life! I love the paradox that the one who loses his life for the sake of the kingdom will find it (see Matthew 10:39). In the same way, *sacrifice*, not self-interest, is the fast lane to joy.

Sacrifice teaches us the joy of putting others first, while it strengthens us to respond decisively to the influence of the Holy Spirit in our lives. A life of self-control and self-denial weeds out a lot of the "wimpiness" in our character. Learning to yield to God and give generously of ourselves is a rather muscular affair that takes guts, like leaping off a high precipice into pitch darkness. It feels risky, but when we can't clearly see what's ahead and we choose to entrust ourselves to God's love, the rewards are just fantastic. It's as if we ventured out into the wilderness with no provisions, away from the comforts of our own desires, to discover mysterious treasures that speak to our hearts like nothing we have ever experienced before.

Before stepping out on the rocky, narrow path, we don't know enough to hope for these amazing gifts, but when we find them, we experience a profound homecoming. To discover our own dignity as daughters of the Most High King—and to share that knowledge with others—is well worth the discomforts and dangers of the journey.

Lost and Found

In 1992, my life hit rock bottom. As I mentioned earlier, I was thirty-three years old when everything suddenly and dramatically turned around. But what I didn't mention was that my whole life was a failure at that point. My career as an actress was going nowhere, and my personal relationships were in tatters. Married for seven years, I desperately wanted children but my body wouldn't cooperate. I was miserable and saw no way out of the pain that seemed to increase, day by day. The bitterness was so intense that it hurt me physically. It occurred to me many times that my anger toward God might eventually kill me outright, and I shook my clenched fist at him whenever I prayed, so deep was the rage against this coldhearted fake who never seemed to answer my prayers.

A product of 1970s college feminism and burdened by experiences of sexual abuse as a young adult, I couldn't separate my own confusion about masculinity from my extremely undeveloped ideas about God. Though I understand now that God is neither male nor female but pure spirit, and that the image of the good "Father" is an endearing clue to how God wants to protect and provide for us, at that terrible time of my life he just seemed like another domineering, heartless man to me. I hated him and wanted nothing to do with him. As far as I was concerned, Catholicism was just a lot of empty baggage, and I was on my way out of the Church forever.

But God, through the Blessed Mother, used unexpected encounters with other women to gently draw me back to the Catholic religion of my childhood, to the sheltering and healing love of Jesus, who would soon remake my ugly life into something beautiful. The women I met along the way each provided a link in the chain that led me to Jesus, and they will always remind me of the beads of a rosary.

I met the first woman when I was killing time before an out-of-town audition. Seemingly by chance, I ran into an old friend in a shop down the road from the theater, and we chitchatted for a little while. She told me about her life and her job, and finally we talked about books. She was very excited to tell me that she was reading a true story about a woman who became the caretaker of a summer cottage on Nantucket Island during the cold, off-season months, in order to live completely alone, without distractions. In the midst of an existential crisis, she had decided to break completely away from her ordinary life to confront her deepest thoughts and desires for the first time. I eagerly purchased a copy and flew through it, fascinated. The idea of escaping ordinary life to uncover the meaning of my existence took hold of my imagination.

I searched for a place where I could be safe, but solitary, for an open-ended retreat of sorts. I called various ashrams and retreat centers in New York, but they were beyond my puny budget. My mother—the next bead in the rosary, if you will—found an inexpensive dormitory on the grounds of a Catholic shrine dedicated to Our Lady of La Salette, where I could stay as long as I wanted for practically nothing. I took a leave from work, bid a hasty farewell to my husband and a few friends, and left with no clear plans for my return.

On the overloaded train from New York's Penn Station to Providence, Rhode Island, the only available seat was next to a young woman, who smiled shyly as I settled next to her. As if our meeting had been arranged, she quickly opened her heart, volunteering the story of her life. Perhaps my desolation was apparent to her and she was moved by concern for a desperate stranger. I was amazed to hear that she had been physically abused by her husband for a number of years, until both their lives were completely transformed by the healing power of...none other than *Jesus Christ*—my nemesis!

As she finished her story, she marveled aloud. She had *never* had the courage to witness to a complete stranger before. As for me, I had never heard anything like her personal love for Christ or her ironclad trust in his power to bring hope to desperate situations. She smiled through her tears as she described how he had rescued her from despair and blessed her beyond measure. I said very little, but the four-hour trip passed quickly.

My mother met me at the train station in Providence. Concerned about my depressed condition, she listened patiently as I wept at a little table in the station's coffee shop and poured out my troubles. Knowing she was there for me, without criticism, was deeply comforting, but I was anxious to be on my way. She gave me a lift to the car rental agency where I had made arrangements, and I drove the rest of the way to the retreat center alone. I registered with a credit card for an open-ended stay and lugged my bags up to a small, bare room. I lay down on the bed, more lonely and frightened than I had ever been in my life. I stayed for eight long days.

I slogged through one agonizingly painful day after another, with nothing to distract me from the despair that had taken hold of my mind. But, for some reason, I couldn't help but pray the rosary. In a particularly desperate moment, months before, I had asked my mother to teach it to me while she was visiting us in Brooklyn. Our family used to pray it together during Lent when I was a kid, but all these years later, I'd forgotten how. Now, I prayed it every day as I walked the grounds of the shrine, unaware of how strange it was to say I rejected God, but to still pray to the Holy Virgin.

Even stranger, daily Mass became the most important event of each day, though I couldn't have told you why. I was still so bitter toward God that I half expected the consecrated Host to burst into flames on my tongue as I received Jesus each day. I was too ignorant to know better, but I was far from being in a state of grace at the time, so I should not have been receiving Communion at all. However, by God's mercy, a women's retreat was held during my stay, and I did make a sacramental confession before I left on the eighth day. (Many years later, my dear friend Pat Gohn would tell me that the "eighth day" is a symbol for eternity.)

One evening during my self-imposed exile, I was restless and went for a walk. There were white, life-sized statues of the Stations of the Cross, as well as other beautiful images, scattered around the grounds of the shrine. Their plaster surfaces reflected the light of the moon, and they seemed to glow in the dark as I moved among them, totally alone. Eventually, I found myself at the top of a flight of stone steps, where a statue of Our Lady of La Salette had been set on a low pedestal so that I could look almost directly into her eyes.

For some reason, it was as if the statue were inviting me to unburden myself, so I spoke to her out loud about everything that was wrong with my life—and every miserable, useless person in it. No one escaped my condemnation or my fury. Like a dam breaking, the agony of my own existential crisis flooded out of me; I complained and cried and exposed my soul completely, every last filthy resentment spilling out at the feet of the Virgin's image. I don't know how much time passed like this, but if anyone heard me wailing away before Our Lady's statue, they surely kept their distance from the crazy woman on the hill.

When there was nothing left, I stood empty before her, my face soaked with bitter tears, my mind exhausted. I just stared at her face in silence. Suddenly, for the first time in my life, words that were not my own were spoken in the depths of my heart. As clearly as if I'd heard them with my ears, I heard her say, "Go see my Son." I froze, astonished at the clarity of her command. But a moment later I obeyed, moving as if in a trance down the stone steps to approach the foot of a much larger staircase leading up to a gigantic crucifix.

Moved by the conviction that the Blessed Mother had, in fact, ordered me to present my needs to Jesus, I gazed up at the huge image of Our Lord on the cross. Mindful that the stairs would have been slowly and reverently mounted by penitent pilgrims on their knees in humble contrition, I disdainfully marched up the steps to the platform at the top, my back straight and my jaw set. When I reached the foot of the cross, I let him have it. If Mary wanted me to see Jesus about my problems, he was going to have to listen to the whole ugly story. Moments before, I could not have imagined such an amazing surge of renewed venom, but I retold every single part of my long, wretched sob story, right there at the base of that cross, weeping as before.

Again I complained, accused, condemned, and cried aloud like a wounded animal. Out it all poured until I was empty of words and drained of emotion. I stood still, glaring up at the face of Christ, tired but ready for him to speak to me or heal me or show me a sign that he actually loved me in spite of everything. But *nothing happened*. Absolutely nothing. Disappointed and feeling foolish, I stalked off to the dormitory, went to bed, and slept through the night.

Yet, when I awoke the next morning, the bitterness was completely gone. It was truly remarkable. I wouldn't say that I felt joyful, but I was lighter and freer than I had been in years. In spite of the lack of spiritual fireworks the night before, it was clear to me that a healing had taken place and that Jesus was responsible. The rest of my stay was increasingly fruitful and included my humble return to the sacrament of reconciliation. I would finally head home, deep into a profound conversion, on the eighth day.

The Blessed Mother's fingerprints were all over my return to Jesus. Women were sent to touch my life and comfort me when I couldn't relate to men. I was led to a holy place of Marian devotion where I could be safe yet experience the solitude necessary for confronting the truth of my life. I discovered that my sins had created a spiritual racket that drowned out the gentle whispers of God to my soul; God had never actually abandoned me, but I needed repentance and sacramental grace to reawaken all that was good and beautiful in me.

One of my favorite books is St. Louis Marie de Montfort's *The Secret of Mary*. In his brief explanation of the spiritual treasures that our souls can receive through the Blessed Mother's powerful influence, St. Louis gives us the image of Mary as the grace-filled "mold" for our souls:

> In that mold none of the features of the Godhead is wanting. Whoever is cast in it and allows himself to be molded, receives all the features of Jesus Christ, true God. The work is done gently, in a manner proportioned to human weakness, without much pain or labor; in a sure manner, free from all illusion, for where Mary is the devil has never had, and never will have, access...[4]

In Mary's soul, God is fully present. So when we conform ourselves to her, we are automatically conformed to God. Her perfect purity and holiness are the models for discipleship that fast-track our souls to heaven. St. Louis describes the state of the soul that easily pours into Mary as being "molten." What a beautiful image of abandonment and trust; the soul becomes liquid, releasing all resistance to transformation and the gentle, perfecting effects of grace.

Since we all fail at times, it's certainly not a perfect record that makes God love us or even makes us beautiful; it is the willingness to turn back to him with a contrite heart, with even the weakest desire to receive the transforming graces that will "make all things new" (Revelation 21:5) and help us to begin again. The continuous falling and rising as we struggle to die to self and become "molten" invigorates our souls and releases a flood of graces—if we accept the humiliation of our spiritual weakness, knowing God's mercy is greater than any fault of ours.

This is why Jesus gives himself to us so powerfully in the sacraments of Eucharist and reconciliation! These two sacraments bless us with sanctifying graces that work together to heal our wounds and strengthen our souls for this precious and holy moment, as well as for the journey ahead. We need these sacraments not just once, but throughout our lives, since our human experience is fraught with distraction, temptation, and suffering.

Our human hearts often crave people and experiences that can never satisfy us, despite what the world tells us—so expect to fall many times a day. We Christians have to be content to creep along, gradually opening to the sacramental graces that alone have the power to reshape and reinvigorate our lives, but as we progress, we quickly notice our lives filling up with hope. Self-imposed limitations or fears that come from our woundedness begin to shrink as our own dreams, gifts, and talents gather strength. As we live increasingly for God, our life's meaning and purpose come into focus. In a confused, lonely, and self-destructive culture, this clarity is a gift without price.

I said earlier that sacrifice is the fast lane to joy, which seems to go against all of our cultural indoctrination. The world tells you to "find yourself," "indulge yourself," "win at all costs," or "be a star!" Yet, from a Christian worldview, sacrificial love makes perfect sense when we think about it logically. If we live only to fit in with others, to curry favor, to accumulate status and wealth, or simply to fulfill our own imperfect plans and cravings, our personal universe will be small and finite. To add insult to injury, all of our plans and projects will die when we do! The psalmist tells us, "Put not your trust in princes, / in a son of man, in whom there is no help. / When his breath departs he returns to his earth; / on that very day his plans perish" (Psalm 146:3–4).

Imagine what we might become by opening our hearts to the enormity of God's love! With renewed courage, we would venture into the wilderness to discover the peace of God's holy purpose for our lives. If we live in the divine will, day-by-day, moment-by-moment, with all of our imperfections yet with a desire to conform ourselves to the Lord, God's plans become our plans; our plans become eternal plans; and our lives continue to bear fruit long after we die.

God's love is a bounty of endless surprises. With unexpected depths of generosity he continually draws us closer, gradually conforming us to his perfection. As our bodies and vocations mature through times of suffering—while religious orders change direction, careers transition or come to an end, children leave the nest, spouses and close friends lose their health, die, or leave us, or our own health declines—we do not lose our relevance to God or our usefulness in helping to heal a broken world.

Even if that world ignores us, we are not less precious to Our Lord. Everything else may change, but he does not. And because he is the source and summit of beauty, the gift of our own interior beauty only increases in value as we continue the process of letting go of the world and embracing the sweetness of the cross.

What the Church Says about Beauty

Holy Mother Church has historically been a great help to us in understanding the concept of beauty properly: as a glimpse of God's glory; as a way of perceiving, inhaling, embracing, and absorbing the intangibles of heaven. God's power speaks through the stirring dramas that unfold all around us in nature, as well as in our human experience. From the soft sighs of infants to the roar of waterfalls, from affectionate kisses to translucent rainbows, the sweet scent of roses to the heady aroma of baking bread, heaven seems only a breath, a touch, or a glance away.

Experience the thrill of running horses, thundershowers, or flocks of geese startled into flight and you will have touched the hem of God's glory. Reflect on the great religious paintings of our Christian heritage and plumb the depths of beauty and meaning found in art: the dance of light and shadow, color and form, symbol and narrative. Like our preliterate Christian brothers and sisters, we are ennobled, edified, and catechized by dramatic visual stories of our faith. Ancient churches resplendent with some of the world's greatest works of art and architecture bring immediacy and drama to God's story of salvation.

Fr. Robert Barron has a wonderful YouTube video called, "Evangelizing Through Beauty."[5] Using as his basis the novel *Brideshead Revisited*, he describes the impact of beauty on the soul:

> Once you're in the building...you're in Brideshead, you're intrigued by the artistic program. Then it begins to work at you. Here's how: You now say, *I want to conform my life to the beauty that I've seen. I want to live in such a way that is congruent to the beauty that I have taken in.* That's how we move from the beautiful to the good. *I want to participate in it.* And that means a change of your life! But now it's not so much someone from the outside telling you what to do, it's *the beautiful* working on you and changing you from the inside...You begin to understand the world that made that beautiful and made that goodness possible. Now you understand from inside the dynamics of the *truth* of the thing.

In the words of many Christian writers, beauty is described as a gateway to truth, and truth a gateway to beauty. God is the source and summit of all that is good, beautiful, and true, which is why experiences of beauty help to prepare our hearts to receive the Gospel. Early Jesuit missionaries understood this and, as they traveled the world winning converts to Christ, they often organized the local people into choirs and orchestras. Dr. Jem Sullivan, an expert on sacred art, explains:

In order to effectively share the Gospel with the native peoples, Jesuit missionaries appealed to their natural affinity for music and their superior musical talents. Evangelists and missionaries understood well that the sheer beauty of sacred music would open hearts, prepare minds for Gospel truths, and uplift and unite the soul to God.[6]

Taking great care and with patient diligence, even the poor and uneducated were trained to sing and play magnificent selections of sacred music. The music, in turn, helped to inspire their newfound Christianity to greater heights of ardor.

When you think of the absence of this kind of devoted, ennobling evangelization and the dearth of beauty offered in most catechetical programs, it is no wonder so much of what we say and do fails to move souls to conversion. Beauty that we can see, hear, and touch speaks of a deeper loveliness, something hidden and divine. We experience this intuitively. Consider the lack of beauty in many modern churches and the lack of modesty and humility in our culture as you meditate on this quote from the great Catholic theologian, Fr. Hans Urs von Balthasar:

> We no longer dare to believe in beauty and we make of it a mere appearance in order the more easily to dispose of it. Our situation today shows that beauty demands for itself at least as much courage and decision as do truth and goodness, and she will not allow herself to be separated and banned from her two sisters without taking them along with herself in an act of mysterious vengeance. We can be sure that whoever sneers at her name as if she were the ornament of a bourgeois past— whether he admits it or not—can no longer pray and soon will no longer be able to love.[7]

It is important to us, in the hurly-burly of our hectic lives, to remember that the power of the beautiful, contemplated in stillness, continues to work its mysterious influence on souls, even today.

Feminine Beauty as a Foretaste of Heaven

I recently discovered a charming old novel (circa 1945), *The World, The Flesh, and Father Smith,* by Scottish writer Bruce Marshall. The title character is a parish priest in love with God. He toils away in a dreary Scottish city full of suffering and sin, and his wisdom and humor rollick through the pages of this delightful, fictional autobiography. His most-quoted (and misappropriated) line is a little jewel, taken from a heated argument that Fr. Smith has with a young woman, a hedonistic atheist, who finds his faith and morals laughable. When she accuses him of replacing sex with religion, he loses his temper and says something very wise (try to imagine him biting off every word in a lovely Scottish brogue): "I still prefer to believe that sex is a substitute for religion and that the young man who rings the bell at the brothel is unconsciously looking for God."[8]

Ponder that thought for a moment. The young man who acts out his lust seeks communion but doesn't know it. The loneliness of his life is only temporarily assuaged through illicit sexual pleasure. His emptiness will return, because he has sought relief through a disordered desire for the gentleness, receptivity, and compassion of women. But what he actually longs for would exceed his wildest dreams. The communion the saints enjoy in heaven is a far greater pleasure, which lasts for all eternity: And yet, because of human blindness, men still knock at brothel doors and women still wait within.

Did you know that each woman's unique physical body expresses her own *individual* feminine soul, that her interior beauty is, in a sense, *spoken* into the world by her body, as well as her actions? The *Catechism of the Catholic Church* teaches that human beings are a unity of body and soul—not just souls temporarily trapped in flesh and bone (see *CCC* 365), but a true unity that amounts to a *single nature.* That nature *images God* (see Genesis 1:27), so it is no error to say that our bodies express the divine, as well as the beauty that is God's gift to every woman.

Even though our bodies will separate from our souls at death, through the power of Christ's resurrection, the bodies of the faithful will one day be raised and glorified, reunited with our souls, incorruptible for all eternity (see *CCC* 997). Our bodies will be without spot or blemish, powerful, and perfect.

Won't we just be *gorgeous*?

Chapter Two

THE SACRED MENTALITY
The Sacramentality of Our Changing Bodies

It is sown a physical body, it is raised a spiritual body. If there
is a physical body, there is also a spiritual body.

—1 Corinthians 15:44

I was sitting in church one Sunday, having a hot flash. I'd been pondering
the strange flushes of heat and perspiration for weeks because they were
coming more frequently and with greater intensity than ever before. I
kept wondering what God was trying to *say* to me. I know that may
sound a bit odd, but I look for meaning in all sorts of things.

Because of the Catholic understanding that our bodies are imbued
with meaning and supernatural dignity, I have come to believe that
everything in my physical experience is part of my conversation with
God.

Body Talk

Of course, our bodies *talk* to us all the time, in a sense. If I am in pain,
God is telling me through the survival mechanisms embedded in my
flesh that I need healing. If I am tired, I need rest; if I am hungry, I need
food—and so on. But even more than a switchboard for maintenance
alerts, the body expresses meaning because it tells us so much about
God's plan for our lives.

Through its developmental stages, physical attributes, capabilities, and natural beauty, the body is eloquent—if we have eyes to see
and ears to hear (pun intended!). As I mentioned above, I had been

pondering the divine message I felt was surely hidden in the meno-pausal symptoms I was experiencing, querying God about it on a daily basis for weeks. My end of the conversation went something like this:

> Lord, what is this heat? What does it mean? The only thing I can think of is that my body is burning away its ability to give life. But that's a depressing thought, and I know you are never depressing. So...what are you trying to tell me?

It was quiet in the church at that particular moment when I began to ask him about it, once again. The heat blazing up through my core was intense, and a film of sweat broke out all over my face and upper body. I opened my jacket and flapped the sides to cool myself, still prayerfully wondering. As I gazed up at the huge crucifix over the altar, it hit me: heat, burning, *fire*...God's fiery love!

Old and New Testament images flooded my mind: Moses removing his shoes to stand on holy ground, as the voice of God speaks to him from the burning bush (see Exodus 3:1–15); a supernatural pillar of fire leading the Israelites through the dark nights of their trek to the prom-ised land (see Exodus 13:21); the rushing wind and tongues of fire that announced the anointing of the Holy Spirit on the apostles, strength-ening and inspiring them and giving birth to the infant Church (see Acts 2)!

Suddenly the heat made sense. I wasn't merely experiencing the end of my fertility; God's burning love was telling me that this "change of life" was a new *anointing*, a whole new beginning. He was speaking to me, leading me, strengthening and inspiring me, and whatever changes he was asking of me were good and holy and beautiful. I knew from that moment that every other change I would face, as I continued to age, would also illuminate my walk with God in some special way.

Suffering as a Sign of Favor

Our bodies continually speak to us of God's presence in our souls, but how do we reconcile the life-giving love of God with physical decline, especially when our aching joints start to slow us down and the ailments and limitations start to pile up? I find it helpful to look at signs of deterioration as a heads-up from God that this life is impermanent, that our time here is preciously limited, and that a healthy Christian ought to focus on the destination as much as the journey. In union with the transcendent power of the cross of Christ, our trials can mark a pathway of sanctification and communion with our suffering Savior.

In Donna-Marie Cooper O'Boyle's book *The Kiss of Jesus: How Mother Teresa and the Saints Helped Me to Discover the Beauty of the Cross,* she relates how Mother Teresa, now Blessed Teresa of Calcutta, once told her, "Suffering is the sharing in the passion of Christ. Suffering is the kiss of Jesus, a sign that you have come so close to Jesus on the Cross that He can kiss you...."[9] There is much truth here. We tend to resist the meaning in our pain because we just want it to stop, but the fruits of our suffering may in fact be the most tender of divine gifts. The saints bear witness.

St. Thérèse of Lisieux died of tuberculosis at the age of twenty-four; St. Anne Catherine Emmerich suffered high fevers and the wounds of Christ's crucifixion (the stigmata) every Friday afternoon for years; before his miraculous healing, St. Peregrine experienced a progressive cancer in one of his legs that caused acute, chronic pain. In each case, the suffering itself preceded a powerful experience of God's glory that had an impact on the world, as well as the saint.

St. Thérèse died young and immediately fulfilled her promise to shower the world with "roses" from heaven. St. Anne Catherine's fevers brought on rich, detailed visions of the hidden life of Jesus and Mary that have been preserved for the Church for all time.[10] St. Peregrine faced amputation of his festering leg just before Jesus appeared to miraculously heal him, making Peregrine a powerful patron for cancer patients.

God can bring good out of anything, so suffering can be looked at as an opportunity for spiritual blessing. If you're rolling your eyes as you shift your aching bones, let me ask you something: Why do you suppose God made us? I mean, what exactly was he thinking right before it all started? Before we can accept that our pain can be a blessing, we really need to start at the very beginning.

The Meaning of Life

The wonderful old Baltimore Catechism[11] tells us that we were made to know and love God, to serve him in this life, and to be happy with him forever in the next. The world's obsession with material goods and self-centered fulfillment aside, God's plan is a radical one full of meaning and glory. But that doesn't really tell us *why* he made us in the first place. Was he lonely? Was he bored? Did he feel incomplete?

When we look at a night sky or at some of the many exquisite photos of nebulas, solar systems, and planets that technology so wondrously reveals to us, we might imagine that God was merely amusing himself when he called each star into existence (see Psalm 33:6); that he felt the need to stretch his creative muscles when he splashed his dazzling creations across the newborn universe; that in the infinite expanse of his solitude he needed something new and exciting to play with, so he conceived a vast multitude of living creatures in various shapes and sizes, culminating in humanity.

Yes, it seems probable that he thoroughly enjoyed willing the created world into existence: that he laughed joyfully as he set off the Big Bang, whooped as he set the swirling Whirlpool Galaxy into motion, or smiled with pleasure as he created the comical duck-billed platypus. It is abundantly clear that he is the master of both majesty and mirth. But if we consider salvation history, we can begin to see with certainty that he didn't do any of it for himself. Compared to all the glories of the universe, God himself is immeasurably more magnificent, humorous, beautiful, and inspiring. What purpose would mere shadows of his glory serve for him?

It is so easy for us to misunderstand the mind of God. "For my thoughts are not your thoughts, / neither are your ways my ways.... / For as the heavens are higher than the earth, / so are my ways higher than your ways / my thoughts than your thoughts" (Isaiah 55:8–9).

Instead of wondering what *need* we fill in the divine heart, it is better to think of God as simply giving us the gift of our lives out of the *goodness* of his heart. The truth is that God's infinite being is so complete and so satisfying to himself that he has no need of us whatsoever. The Trinity is the ultimate communion of persons, a family delightful beyond our imaginings. We exist because God is infinitely beautiful, infinitely good, and overflowing with a love that seeks to share itself. When he made us and placed us in this glittering created world, it was an act of pure generosity.

Sacraments and Sacramentality

Think for a moment of anything stunningly beautiful that has ever taken you completely out of yourself. Perhaps it was a newborn baby or a thunderstorm, a breaching whale or a magnificent symphony. Try to remember how it made you feel in the moment when you stopped thinking and just let yourself be lifted up and carried away.

When this happens to me, I feel limitless and radiant, as if God's bright hand had touched me and given me a glimpse of my truest, holiest purpose. Though the experience may be fleeting, I long to act on the glorious sense of discovery that is rising inside me, to hold on to it and make it a part of my life, forever. As John O'Donohue says in his book *Beauty: The Invisible Embrace*, "When we experience beauty, we feel called. The Beautiful stirs passion and urgency in us and calls us forth from aloneness into the warmth and wonder of an eternal embrace...in an instant it can awaken under the layers of the heart a forgotten brightness."[12]

The beauty of nature is just one way that God calls us to virtue and self-donation, displaying his incomparable artistry for our edification. He calls us to follow his example as best we can, relying on his grace to buoy and inspire us, to use ourselves for the good of others by expressing our own lives beautifully and generously. The loveliness all around us has a genuine *sacramentality*, which means that in a very real and intentional way, beauty speaks to us of God's presence. Sacramentality and sacraments, however, are two very different things.

Sacraments are efficacious signs of spiritual realities. The ritual of the sacrament actually accomplishes what it represents, because in each sacrament, Jesus personally effects a spiritual change through the ritual actions of a priest or deacon.[13] For example, through flowing water and the invocation of the Trinity, baptism irrevocably marks our souls as Catholic, cleansing our souls of original sin, bringing us into the family of God, and preparing us to receive the Gospel.

In the sacrament of reconciliation, we are cleansed and healed, forgiven by God through the words of absolution spoken by a priest, who stands *in persona Christi* (in the person of Christ). Through bread and wine consecrated in the hands of the priest, Holy Communion plunges us into the one-time sacrifice of the cross, nourishing our souls with the Body, Blood, Soul, and Divinity of Jesus Christ. Each of the seven sacraments was instituted by Jesus Christ, and each of them is a gift that helps us to point our lives homeward, to heaven.

To make the distinction clearer, while sacraments actually *cause* the spiritual effects that they signify, "sacramentality" is the quality inherent in creation that has the power to open our hearts to the presence of God. Like a beacon shining in the night, the sacramentality of the created world breaks through our wordly preconceptions and reminds us that God is infinitely beautiful, creative, and complex; that we are loved boundlessly; and that we ourselves are called to love without limits.

A World of Illiteracy

What God writes in the skies, the oceans, the wind, and the rain provides a glimpse of his purpose for our lives, rooted in his incomparably generous love. Since we are made in his image, this love gives meaning to our lives, so it makes sense to be on the lookout for signs of his presence in the world around us. In fact, recent scientific discoveries point resolutely to the existence of our Creator, revealing all the structures of the universe's intelligent design by a "someone" with a purpose and a plan.

Writing for the *Wall Street Journal* on Christmas Day 2014, author Eric Metaxas described the sheer, astronomical impossibility of the universe without God. Citing the supposedly random accomplishment of a mathematically inconceivable multitude of subtle, interdependent astrophysical conditions needed for the universe to even exist—never mind for the earth to support life—he uses up-to-date research to demonstrate the futility of resistance to the reality of God. Facts and numbers, not philosophies, are convincing a growing number of scientists—even astrophysicists who formerly had deeply-held atheistic beliefs—that a Creator must, in fact, exist.[14]

Throughout history, the human heart has been capable of discerning God's presence in the beauty, balance, and intricacy of nature, experiencing an understandable awe when confronted with the delicacy and individuality of everything from souls to snowflakes. Sadly, in modern times, science and technology have been distorted into objects of worship, and many people have set their hopes on a futuristic, manmade utopia in which discomfort and suffering will supposedly be eliminated for good. Religion has been chucked wholesale, considered superfluous in the light of humanity's impressive accomplishments. It's wonderfully ironic that science and technology are now becoming allies to faith.

Furthermore, suffering has not, in fact, been banished by human achievements, and the egoistic drive to eliminate God from our view of the universe and replace his glory with our own paltry successes has failed to result in greater peace, hope, or love. The fad in our times is to apply our own personal meaning to everything, a designer reality in which the goal is to have a personal "truth," which can then peacefully coexist with everyone else's personal truth. On the surface, it all seems rather friendly and sophisticated. But look deeper and you discover lives without any solid meaning or moral standards, subject to all sorts of pressures and fluctuations, because if *everything* is true, then *nothing* is true.

Witness the proliferation of spiritually destructive New Age practices that have thrust our sophisticated society backward into the superstitions of the ancient pagan world. Resurgent occult influences like fortune-telling and séances, earth worship, witchcraft, and a fascination with reincarnation have blended together in a consumer's paradise of pick-and-choose "beliefs," a smorgasbord of junk spirituality that proudly eschews anything "organized."

Fortunately for us, we have the Magisterium of the Catholic Church, which, with the constant help of the Holy Spirit, has guarded the faith and morals of Catholics for more than two thousand years. More recently, we have been blessed by a remarkable set of teachings—introduced by St. John Paul II—called the "theology of the body." By more profoundly illuminating the sacramentality of our bodies, this theology helps us to live lives of great beauty and meaning in a world insensible to God's exquisite language of love. Catholic author Emily Stimpson sums it up this way:

> John Paul II's response to that problem was to offer the world a reading lesson. The theology of the body is like Hooked on Phonics for the sacramental worldview, offering the contemporary mind a step-by-step lesson plan for how to read the world rightly once more. It does that by taking men back to the beginning, back to the Garden, where it uses the human body as the starting point for rediscovering the meaning inherent in all creation.[15]

The Theology of the Body

Over the course of about five years (1979–1984), St. John Paul II gave a series of weekly public talks in St. Peter's Square devoted to the meaning of the human person through a biblical understanding of the body and human sexuality. These extraordinary presentations, now known collectively as the "theology of the body," are highly regarded throughout much of the Christian world, and the series has since been translated, analyzed, disseminated, and propagated widely. This goldmine of timeless Gospel values can be summed up very simply: The call to live selflessly is profoundly embedded, not only in the world around us, but in our own bodies—no matter what our age or condition.

The Bible tells us in the book of Genesis, that "In the beginning," human beings were innocent, happy, and naked. Ancient Jewish writers pointed out the lack of clothing because, in their times and in their scriptures, nakedness was very often linked with shame. But in the Garden of Eden, things were different. Nakedness, they tell us, started out as a joy, not an embarrassment. Adam and Eve were made *for* each other and not meant to be alone; their bodies fit together perfectly, enabling them to reflect God's creative powers through procreation.

The Garden was an exceptionally joyful place. The first people served each other naturally, without hesitation or thought of self. You know the old saying, "You can't give what you haven't got"? Adam and Eve were in complete possession of themselves, which made it possible for them to give themselves freely and totally to each other. Their acceptance of each other, likewise, was complete, so they had no fear at all of being humiliated or rejected.

The powerful, but tender, attraction between our first parents was completely without shame because it was at once erotic and reverent, physical and spiritual—as it was meant to be. The "nuptial" or "marital" meaning of their bodies, which was fulfilled in generous self-donation, was unrestricted and unsullied. We think of God as "Trinitarian" because we believe that he is a harmonious communion of three Persons: the Father, the Son, and the Holy Spirit. Adam and Eve's true and holy communion with God and with each other was also in perfect harmony and overflowed with the joy of that perfection. The marital union of the two spouses became a living metaphor for the Trinity, an image of God's nature, with its capability of producing a third life, in the person of a child.

It was not until Adam and Eve disobeyed God out of a prideful desire to be like him that their bodies started to suffer the consequences of sin, including pain, sickness, and aging. Rather than master the temptation to put themselves above God, they gave in. Disastrously, by seeking something for themselves, they lost the holy freedom they had enjoyed together, the true self-possession necessary to give of themselves completely. They had turned away from God, the source of that freedom. Their nakedness now caused them shame because for the first time they looked at each other and lusted. Horrified, they were suddenly afraid of God and alienated from each other—and even from their own bodies.

Fascinatingly, one of the teachings of the theology of the body is that shame is a sign that the goodness of God is still present in us. We instinctively protect the most sensitive and holy parts of the human body by covering them up. Because human beings are prone to lust, we veil what is sacred in order to increase reverence for what should remain innocent and pure. Modesty protects our life-generating powers, which image the creativity of God, and expresses the innate knowledge that our bodies are good and should not be treated otherwise.

The Feminine Genius

In the mid-nineteenth century, women's suffrage began as a universal human rights movement that tackled both the abolition of slavery and the acquisition of women's property rights, culminating in 1920 with the American woman's right to vote. Since then, the modern women's movement has brokered considerable advances, including laws against sexual harassment, measures to promote equal wages for equal work, access to educational and athletic funding, and federal regulations requiring deadbeat fathers to support their families.

So often a great blessing to the progress of women, the authentic heart of feminism has, in my opinion, declined, in recent years. Rather than embracing all women and supporting them in speaking for themselves—as individuals with a wide variety of personal views and values—much of the contemporary women's movement seeks to dominate and intimidate women into adopting radical liberal views:

rejecting their fertility, seeing promiscuity as a right, and treating religion as a hindrance to progress.

One of the closing statements of the Second Vatican Council sent an urgent message to the world and set the stage for a more serious dialogue about the need for an authentic feminine presence in society:

> But the hour is coming, in fact has come, when the vocation of woman is being achieved in its fullness, the hour in which woman acquires in the world an influence, an effect and a power never hitherto achieved. That is why, at this moment when the human race is under-going so deep a transformation, women impregnated with the spirit of the Gospel can do so much to aid mankind in not falling.[16]

St. John Paul II's apostolic letter, *Mulieris Dignitatem*,[17] promoted the Church's long-held vision of equality between the sexes, highlighting the special gifts of women: generosity, receptivity, maternity, and sensitivity. Illuminating and applauding the natural feminine gifts and their critical importance to the health of civilization, John Paul II dubbed these qualities "the feminine genius." He further clarified the Church's different-but-equal view of the two sexes, spurring a rebirth of vibrant Catholic thought on the role of women in Church and society that has been taken up, in turn, by Pope Benedict XVI and Pope Francis. Catholic women took note, and they have joyfully embraced the task of unpacking and disseminating these beautiful teachings to the world.[18]

Like many American women, I grew up listening to the secular media's distorted claims against the Church as being misogynistic, so it was exciting when I later discovered the truth: that a true and ardent love of femininity is almost ubiquitous in Catholicism. In fact, any Catholic discussion of the Church utilizes feminine imagery. We recognize the Church *herself* as the "Bride of Christ" and as "Mother Church" because she provides sanctuary and spiritual nourishment to her children.

Catholicism has always elevated the feminine, protecting women more than any other belief system by firmly upholding the sanctity of marriage vows and obediently taking as its top mandate the call for all Christians to protect and provide for the poor—including widows and orphans. In fact, throughout the history of the Church, much of our spirituality has sprung from a proper reverence and love for the Blessed Virgin Mary, the Mother of Jesus, our King.

To ancient Jews, the mother of the king was the most powerful woman in society. Called the Queen Mother, she was the only woman who was permitted to sit at the king's right hand. Not even his wife was so esteemed. So it was natural for Jesus to elevate his own Mother with the highest possible honor in heaven. And on the simplest level, in obedience to the Father's laws, he honors his Mother. We should do no less.

Sometimes we worry that loving Mary will somehow hinder our love for Jesus. But the fact is that we can never love her as much as Jesus does, so we should try to love her as much as we can. At the annunciation, the archangel Gabriel called Mary "full of grace," revealing her as the holiest being God has ever created, above the entire heavenly host in perfection and beauty. She is the Queen of Heaven, Mother of the Church, and Mother of Divine Grace, among her many titles.

Mary has even been called "the paradise of God," because it was within her that God chose to dwell and to be incarnated. She is the gateway through which Jesus passed from heaven to earth.[19] He entrusted to her his very being, body and spirit, for nine blessed months and beyond. We are invited to image the life of Christ and follow his example by relying upon her maternal love and protection as we journey back to heaven.

Widespread devotion to the rosary and ecclesial approval of many Marian apparitions have brought traditional Catholic culture right into the Immaculate Heart of the most beautiful woman who ever lived. Called the Apostle of the Apostles, she is the premier role model for all who would faithfully follow Jesus Christ.

What's New about the "New" Feminism?

Recently, something called "The New Feminism" has been getting quite a bit of press, both in print and online. An expression coined by St. John Paul II in his encyclical *Evangelium Vitae*, the New Feminism is about helping women to live and express Gospel values more effectively in the Church and in the world, by recognizing their own authentic gifts and mission.[20]

It remains to be seen what new initiatives will arise from this more recent conversation, but as the mother of a teenage daughter, I am thrilled that our Holy Father, Pope Francis, has called for a more profound theology of women in the Church. His cry for progress recalls St. John Paul II's *Letter to All Women*[21]:

> I am convinced that the secret of making speedy progress in achieving full respect for women and their identity involves more than simply the condemnation of discrimination and injustices, necessary though this may be. Such respect must first and foremost be won through an effective and intelligent campaign for the promotion of women, concentrating on all areas of women's life and beginning with a universal recognition of the dignity of women.[22]

For women to see themselves as God sees them—beautiful, influential, vital to the health of the Church—our lives need to more clearly embody the virtues that women most naturally exemplify. We should never bow to pressure from false guides who would have us negate our femininity as if it were a burdensome mistake. Authentic femininity can be powerfully expressed in any of a multitude of callings and professions. We women, in all our dignity and giftedness, are created to have a necessary and lasting impact on the world, through our individual responses to God's call to our sensitive, generous, receptive, and maternal hearts.

And of course, our feminine beauty is sacramental, a visible reminder of God's self-donating love. Gorgeous curves aside, with our natural receptivity in both the spiritual and physical realms and our enthusiasm for creating sanctuaries of love, learning, and peace, our femininity actually exemplifies the proper relationship of the soul to God.

Even men, spiritual writers tell us, assume a feminine attitude in relationship to God. The soul is not taken by force, but falls in love and becomes receptive, the way a bride is receptive to her groom.

So many popes and saints have enjoyed a deep and transformative relationship with the Blessed Virgin Mary, "our tainted nature's solitary boast."[23] Our Lady is the perfect example of both feminine perfection and Christian discipleship. Mary's example of heroic virtue, generous receptivity, and a will exercised courageously in the service of God has become a blueprint for sanctity throughout the history of the Church, for both men and women.

Dr. Alice von Hildebrand, the wife of the late Dietrich von Hildebrand,[24] wrote a beautiful little book called *The Privilege of Being a Woman*, which illuminates the many features of our femininity that are unique, beautiful, and profoundly Christian.[25] As she explains, our feminine "weakness" (compared to the generally greater physical strength of the male body) images the weakness and vulnerability chosen by Our Lord. Jesus deigned to stoop down to the earth and assume human flesh in the form of a helpless human infant dependent upon the care of human beings, rather than appearing in all his divine glory to impress or dominate us. Even in his adult life, he appealed to us through gentleness and a willingness to serve: healing, cleansing, and feeding others wherever he went.

Paradoxically, his humility—which the world would describe as weakness—is a mark of his great strength. Likewise, through the very characteristics that are integral to our feminine beauty—our receptivity, gentleness, and compassion—we image the all-powerful King of the Universe. Jesus was never a careerist or a glory-monger; he did not demand to be hailed as a king or lauded as a hero. He came to live among us, to suffer with us, and to serve us from the heart. He came to teach us how to love.

The Sacramentality of Aging

As I suggested at the beginning of this chapter, our bodies are an integral part of our conversation with God. My way of understanding that conversation is just that: my way. God uses everything to speak with us, including our imaginations, Scripture, the teachings of the Church, and the people in our lives, establishing patterns that aid us in discerning his voice in our lives over time. In my case, if I take a moment to look more closely at almost anything, I can sense the gentle voice of God whispering to my soul.

Sunlight filtering through trees, creating a dappled pattern on the ground, tells me that God is there in the light and in the shadows, that he is present in every moment of both joy and sorrow. He is there whether we see him or not, whether we choose to travel his bright, rugged, narrow way or choose the dark, easy way that is wide and full of the fury of the world.

Even in the innocence and devotion of my dog, I see a reminder from heaven to stay simple and devout! I call our funny little canine "a smile from heaven" because God uses him to make us laugh every single day, no matter what else is going on in our lives. Everywhere I look, it seems that God is sending me coded messages.

So, it's natural for me to see a hot flash as part of God's secret code! I even find symbolism in night sweats, sleeplessness, menopausal morning sickness, aches and pains, and mood swings. You see, when I wake up at night and can't go back to sleep, I feel called to pray for those who are in sunlight on the other side of the world—people who may be suffering, longing for the touch of God's grace, or having doubts that he exists.

When I wake bathed in sweat, I think of my baptism and the privilege of being a child of God, and I praise him for this great gift. When I experience hormonal morning sickness, I think of women in crisis pregnancies and pray for their needs. When I look at my wrinkles and sagging skin, I see the impermanence of this life that makes way for the eternal beauty of the life to come. Thinning bones can be viewed as a sign that gravity's hold on me is waning, that I am slowly being lifted up to God!

I figure that everything belongs to God, so he can use it to speak to us if we are open. I do *not* think I am always correct about what God is saying. But I know that he is tender and kind, and that he blesses my fumbling, ordinary efforts to discern.

Sometimes it is the absence of any clear message that touches me. When I look up at the Eucharist, I note the invisibility of God's beauty, so humbly hidden from view, yet so powerful and life-changing in its mysteries. When the humility of God strikes my heart in this way, I resolve to accept the feelings of invisibility that come with being an aging woman in a culture that overlooks and disregards us. Our beauty, too, is real, even if the world can't see it.

After all, we are mature Christian women. We don't need the approval of a demented culture! We walk in love, through grace. We *have* the treasures our souls seek; we have the beauty of heaven in our minds and souls. Our God gifts us with femininity in all its glory, in its various stages of life, like steps on a stairway to heaven.

If we focus on getting to heaven every day, each phase of our lives, no matter how challenging, will be revealed as a gift in some way. We need to prayerfully pull aside the delicate wrappings that hide the meaning of each human experience and try our best to peek inside.

Chapter Three

Fog Bound

Hope and Help for Your Aging Brain

I will not forget you.

Behold, I have graven you on the palms of my hands.

—Isaiah 49:15–16

God might never forget me, but, for a while, I couldn't guarantee I wouldn't forget *him*. I'd heard of middle-aged brain fog, but this was ridiculous. Around the one-year point of menopause, my short-term memory sharply declined. Again and again, I missed appointments that were important to me because I forgot to consult my planner—or because I did check it, but the information slipped my mind.

I was losing my glasses and other personal items more than usual, and sometimes, while driving, I would suddenly realize I had no idea where I was going. For a heart-stopping moment, I'd be dazed and searching my memory for clues to my destination. While each incident probably only lasted a second or two, it constituted a major change in cognitive function for me and set off alarm bells. *What on earth is happening to my brain?* I wondered. *Surely this can't be normal.*

Ultimately, I stumbled on a nutritional solution that provided dramatic improvement, but I'd like to share the process that I went through, in hopes that it will help you or someone you love. After the sections on brain health, I'll offer some techniques for keeping your spiritual life on track as your brain ages.

Searching for Answers in the Fog

First let's define "brain fog." Whether the cause is hormonal, dietary, or drug-induced, sudden and disturbing episodes of cognitive disorientation sometimes hit without warning, resulting in memory loss and a reduction in the ability to focus. Ask any woman over fifty if she has ever had such a lapse and you are likely to get a hearty laugh of recognition and some hair-raising stories. These stories are amusing only in retrospect, however. When it's happening to you, brain fog can seem to signal the end of life as you know it.

When my cognitive problems were at their worst, I dove into the Internet to query "symptoms of dementia" and found three signs that described me perfectly:[26]

1. Memory loss that disrupts daily life
2. Confusion with time or place
3. Misplacing things and losing the ability to retrace steps

In a panic, I turned my attention to medical websites that addressed similar issues characteristic of menopause. Fortunately, much of what is written about menopausal "brain fog" or "brain fatigue" assuaged my concerns. Experiences like mine are widely reported by women in perimenopause, menopause, and beyond, and they can fade with time.

Of course, there are a lot of different causes for sudden declines in cognitive function. Hormones play a major part during the changes of midlife, but for those of us past menopause, certain common drugs can also cause side effects that mimic dementia.

Sleeping pills are well known for causing mental lapses, and a host of other common drugs are similarly implicated: statin drugs, used for lowering cholesterol, are apparently notorious for causing memory failure. Also, antihistamines, antibiotics, antidepressants, antipsychotics, antispasmodics, and antihypertensives—the "anti" drugs, as one writer puts it[27]—have been found to have an impact on memory and mental clarity in some users. Each person reacts individually to chemicals, however, so what causes one person trouble might be totally fine for another.

Adverse reactions depend on the unique, genetically-determined body chemistry of each consumer, so some pharmacy schools recently started offering students genetic testing to determine their own likely responses to various types of drugs.[28] The process is meant to educate students in the use of individualized drug therapies and, one hopes, make them better pharmacists. I find this attention to the individual encouraging, since it suggests a trend away from the knee-jerk writing of prescriptions for every symptom and a departure from a one-size-fits-all checklist. Human beings are not machines that can all be "repaired" in precisely the same way.

Popular recommendations for alleviating brain fog include: extra sleep, lowering stress levels, and—in extreme cases—estrogen supplementation. I wasn't sleeping very well when the "fog" first rolled into my life, so I started taking short naps in the late afternoons to try to refresh my exhausted mind. I couldn't do much about my stress levels, but I brought it to prayer and did my best to live with an attitude of trust.

My other symptoms—hot flashes, night sweats, and morning sickness—were not severe enough to consider hormone replacement therapy (HRT), though I did discuss this with a specialist. If it had come to that, I would have been open to the newer, more gentle "cooperative HRT" options, which use natural, bio-identical hormones. They appear to be safer than the synthetic HRT most often prescribed by obstetricians—a therapy widely believed to increase the risk of blood clots, heart attacks, and breast, liver, and cervical cancer.

According to Catholic physician Dr. Anne Nolte of the Gianna Center[29] in New York City, who prescribes the more natural, alternative HRT in her practice, the benefits of bio-identical hormones are "very effective and life-changing for some women." Proper use can alleviate severe symptoms of brain fog, mood swings, and night sweats. The hope that cooperative HRT is safer in terms of the side effects and health risks is supported by small, preliminary studies. However, Dr. Nolte is cautious, only prescribing cooperative HRT when symptoms are so severe that a woman's life is becoming unmanageable.

Your Brain Is What You Eat

I was starting to get a handle on the medical consensus but still was wiped out and fogged in. In a subsequent query about brain health, I found an article on a controversial new book[30] by a medical doctor who claimed that eating grains contributed dramatically to the decline of brain function. I love breads, pastas, cookies, and granola—and I already had been eating gluten-free alternatives. I ordered a copy of *Grain Brain* and read it avidly, eventually trying some of the recommended recipes and then adapting them to my own tastes.

As a result, I shifted from my daily gluten-free granola to a bowl of chopped, mixed nuts, topped off with cinnamon, ground flax, chia seeds, and shredded coconut. I covered it all with almond or rice milk and fresh fruit. It was luscious and satisfying, so I was able to cut out all grains for several weeks without much suffering.

Almost immediately, I experienced an increase in energy and stamina, followed by a marked improvement in mental clarity. My daily naps evaporated, because I was much less tired, and my productivity improved along with my morale. Even though I occasionally do eat some grains, I maintain a reduced intake overall, and my memory and energy levels remain pretty stable.

Note: I am absolutely not saying that going grain-free is the answer to every cognitive issue. I'm not even certain it was the solution to mine. Since I have always eaten a fair amount of fruit, it's quite likely that something in the nuts and seeds had been missing from my diet, previously—possibly folate and/or omega-3 fatty acids, both of which have been linked to brain health and are abundant in nuts and seeds.

Whatever the reason for the remarkable improvement, my energy levels soared and inspired me to join a gym. Working out regularly, along with regular chiropractic care, has caused my vitality and concentration to again leap upward. The combination of these wholesome new habits may be the reason for a noticeable improvement in my immune system and digestive tract, as well. When I feel a little sickness coming on, it usually lasts only briefly, and symptoms of irritable bowel syndrome (IBS) have virtually disappeared. One helpful change led to another, and what seemed to be a swift decline into aging made way for a genuine renewal of my health.

I have long been aware of my own food sensitivities to gluten and dairy products, so adapting my diet to improve my health is nothing new for me. A few years ago, a friend of mine mentioned that she was eating gluten-free, and when she revealed that it was to support healthy thyroid function, I was intrigued. I'd been on daily medications for a hyperactive thyroid for a few years at that point, so I eliminated about 90 percent of the gluten from my diet, not expecting much. Within two months of this shift, my endocrinologist pronounced me to be in complete remission, confirmed the anecdotal link between gluten sensitivity and thyroid issues, and helped wean me off all medications. I've had no thyroid issues since 2011. Again, this is personal, anecdotal information, not a medical recommendation that should be applied without careful inquiry.

Personally, I'd rather tweak my habits than take medication, though I value medical science and its amazing diagnostic and surgical capabilities. Each pharmaceutical drug has both an upside and a downside, and along with its benefits come side effects and risks that must be weighed. Most of the time, going the natural route has worked well for me. Overall, I'm a big believer that, when it comes to our health, we need to be cryptographers; cracking the code for our best possible diet and lifestyle should be a gradual, lifelong pursuit.

I offer a gentle warning: What we discover through experimentation and research sometimes leads us to make choices contrary to the traditions and cultural wisdom of our families and friends, so be ready for some blowback from your inner circle. For example, going gluten-free might really annoy your Italian mother! Reducing grains might mean occasionally saying a sweet but firm no to your best friend's lovely baked goods. Those who love you and want the best for you may pressure you to take medicine for every ache and pain; they don't want to see you suffer, so it's understandable. Try to see it that way and be compassionate.

But, while we should always be kind, we shouldn't let anyone else's habits or preferences stop us from striving to grow stronger and healthier, at any age. Alternative foods and recipes are widely available online and in a huge variety of cookbooks. If you enjoy cooking, it can actually be fun to explore. However you feel about the discomforts and challenges of questioning the status quo, I offer this prayer for you:

> Lord, bless this woman in this moment. Give her your holy peace and a deep and abiding joy. Show her, one step at a time, simple ways to open to the abundant health and strength that you desire for her life. If she is chronically ill or disabled, I beg you to give her the courage to live in hope as she researches

her options, asks for help when she needs it, and entrusts each day to the outpouring of grace that accompanies every act of faith. Thank you for the people in this unique and beautiful woman's life. May they be inspired to support her as she grows in grace and wisdom. May they learn humility and a sense of wonder from her lively curiosity and patient perseverance. Amen.

Alzheimer's Prevention

Dr. David Snowdon, author of the book *Aging with Grace*, wrote: "Many people still believe that, as we age, our minds wear out, and that if we live long enough, we will inevitably become demented. This is a myth."[31]

One of the best books I've read on brain health, *Aging with Grace* contains Dr. Snowdon's famous account of his landmark, decades-long Alzheimer's study of the School Sisters of Notre Dame. Snowdon was able to obtain access to the personal records of the community's members and enjoyed warm and lasting friendships with many of the nuns.

The sisters were an ideal population for his epidemiological study because they had so much in common. They all had similar lifestyles, healthy diets, and good medical care because they lived in community, reducing the variables that might otherwise complicate his analysis. Also, the sisters were inspiringly selfless in helping him and his team to better understand Alzheimer's disease, which touched Snowdon's heart very deeply. Amazingly, many of the nuns willed their brains to his ongoing research, and the findings were exciting.

By doing an in-depth analysis of their brains and their medical and personal histories, and by reviewing the results of cognitive tests conducted by his team at various points in the sisters' lives, Dr. Snowdon was able to isolate certain variables that dramatically affect brain health in the final decades of life. Here are a few of the most important ones:

- Linguistic development in early life helps to protect the brain from Alzheimer's disease.
- Higher levels of education in the adult years are similarly protective of brain function in the long term.
- Social interaction helps to maintain mental clarity, whereas isolation causes a diminishment of mental powers.
- Too much dependence on helpers in old age speeds cognitive loss, while situations that encourage independence help maintain and sometimes restore mental well-being.
- Nutrition and exercise matter.
- Positive mental attitudes, closely linked with religious faith, are linked with healthy brains and a greater capacity to heal.

Let's start with early education. Since each nun had been told to write a brief autobiography during her novitiate, Dr. Snowdon was able to study hundreds of these early writings to get a snapshot of each woman's intellectual development at around the age of twenty.

He found that sisters who were well-read and educated in their formative years were able to express complex thoughts through the written word, while others were less developed and described their lives in more basic terms. For instance, one sister might have written, "My mother is a nurse and my father is a farmer. I have three brothers." Yet another might have said, "In a small valley, our farm sprawls across a hundred acres of verdant land, producing enough barley and corn to support our lively family of five boys and two girls."

When the writing samples were compared to the cognitive test results of each nun, it was clear that the ability to express complex thoughts at a young age was strongly indicative of good brain health in their seventies, eighties, nineties, and beyond. Likewise, the writing samples exhibiting less-developed tools of expression were strongly predictive of cognitive decline in later years.

Please understand that Dr. Snowdon did not discover that *intelligence itself* protects our brains from Alzheimer's; but *education* seems to help! Stimulating the brain with rigorous learning has an invigorating effect, just as regular exercise strengthens our hearts. It was also found that women who continued to challenge themselves intellectually by seeking advanced degrees and by continuing to grow in their work through midlife and beyond were also far more likely to have strong brain function in their later years.

Astonishingly, it was discovered that the majority of the more educated nuns, even those whose autopsied brains exhibited extensive physical signs of advanced Alzheimer's disease, maintained mental clarity throughout their lives. Many of them lived into their nineties with no significant signs of cognitive decline.

For those whose later years were fraught with chronic physical illness, again, mental stimulation was key to supporting brain health. In fact, when it was discovered through Dr. Snowdon's work that isolation was detrimental to their brains, the order started reintegrating disabled, elderly nuns into the life of their convents. Cafeteria access and living arrangements were adjusted to make sure that every nun felt a part of the community, and routines were adapted to encourage independence in those who could still walk unassisted or feed and dress themselves.

The results were immediate and positive, with declining elderly women brightening and reconnecting with life in visible and beautiful ways.[32] Clearly, human beings are neither meant to be alone nor to be totally dependent on others. Staying as involved as possible in families and communities is an important factor in ensuring brain health.

Probably the most amazing woman I know is my mother-in-law, who, in her nineties, is still inquisitive, sociable, involved in her parish, and a voracious reader. With no advanced degrees, she was, however, a wartime nurse and has always enjoyed a healthy appetite for informal learning.

If we find ourselves in a bit of a rut, helping out in church ministries, volunteering in the community, joining clubs, and organizing social opportunities to enjoy with others are just a few of the ways we can ramp up our social involvement and clear out the cobwebs. Bible studies, book clubs, crossword puzzles, card games, and other enjoyable mental challenges can provide stimulation to our aging brains that will help keep them youthful and vital.

In fact, any activity that oxygenates or stimulates the brain helps keep your mind strong. So, exercise as much as you can, according to your condition and circumstances. Naturally, you should check with your doctor before beginning any new program, especially if it's been a while since you've taken on a physical challenge of that sort. Use common sense and make changes gradually, but don't be tied to anyone's expectations based merely on your chronological age. You are unlike any other person on the planet. Find what works for you and don't be afraid to move outside your comfort zone.

Here's a nice little tidbit for you: Remember my nutty breakfast? Dovetailing his own research with a major British study on nutrition, Dr. Snowdon confirmed that folate (B9) deficiencies contribute to the onset of dementia in adults.[33] Folic acid, which is often added to breads, cereals, and citrus juices, is a synthetic form of this essential nutrient. The study showed that folic acid is helpful to a degree but that folate is best acquired naturally, through consumption of (among other food sources) dark, leafy greens, asparagus, broccoli, citrus fruits, beans, avocados, liver, and—you guessed it—nuts and seeds.

Finally, a positive mental outlook based in religious faith is a big plus. The nun study showed that, while it is not necessary to be blindly optimistic in our thinking, it is good for our brains to ponder upbeat, hopeful thoughts, and to have an enthusiastic attitude toward life.[34] Prayerful people have an advantage here, since our life of faith brings gifts of faith, hope, and love to our frail human souls, and communion with the qualities of the divine brings us joy and healing, even if life has taught us bitter lessons. Dr. Snowdon concurs:

> My sense is that profound faith, like a positive outlook, buffers the sorrows and tragedies that all of us experience. Evidence is now starting to accumulate from other studies that prayer and contemplation have a positive influence on long-term health and may even speed the healing process. We do not need a study to affirm their importance to the quality of life.[35]

For those of us already in midlife and beyond, it is beneficial to continue to go deeper into our faith and to seek ways to engage and challenge our own minds, both socially and intellectually. In every choice we make, every day and in every moment, we impact the welfare of our brains.

According to bestselling author Nicholas Carr, whose 2010 book *The Shallows* analyzes contemporary studies on the human brain, our neural pathways continuously adapt to the various ways in which we live our lives.[36] "Neuroplasticity," as this fluctuating quality of the brain has been dubbed, is an exciting discovery, revealing that our neural circuits are in constant flux: The parts of our brain that are used and challenged grow stronger, while unused areas of our brains wither and can eventually die off. In short, we hardwire our brains through actions that are repeated consistently, over time, which is why old habits are so hard to break and new routines take time to feel easy and natural.

What we don't use of our brains, we quickly lose, says Carr, but, on the bright side, it is possible to protect our brain health and even to bring our levels of cognitive function back to healthy levels. It bears repeating that true dementia is not a normal symptom of aging, and any signs of cognitive decline should be investigated thoroughly so that an individual strategy can be created for each unique person. New habits may be difficult to establish, but they are not impossible. We can greatly improve the odds of enjoying healthy, vibrant minds at every stage of life, if we're willing to work at it.

Brain Fog and Spirituality

Women often sense a need to simplify our prayer lives as we get older. Part of the reason is that we have less energy, so we are attracted to a more organic approach, perhaps cultivating a companionable awareness of God throughout our day. But, as we've been discussing, it can sometimes be a frustrating struggle just to focus. Dementia and physical health aside, as we age, many women experience some loss of concentration during prayer. The depths of spirituality we might once have enjoyed may seem more elusive, as we experience periods of ill health, exhaustion, or chronic stress.

It's been helpful to me to devise some simple strategies to keep my spiritual life on track. Yours might look very different, but here are some thoughts based on my own experiences:

For me, it takes humility to accept each day as a gift. It means I have to pause and appreciate it, to value it, and to give praise and thanks to God for my life. It's harder to squander a day that I've just been pondering with gratitude.

I start each day by praying a "Come Holy Spirit" prayer and "The Prayer of St. Gertrude for the Holy Souls," then reading a chapter of the New Testament. If I will not be able to make it to Mass that day,

I will also add the "Spiritual Communion" prayer. (The text of each of these can be found online.)[37]

I once had a Protestant colleague who used to laugh at the way Catholic liturgies require us to sit, stand, kneel, sit, stand, kneel, and so on. She jokingly called it "Catholic calisthenics." But often, when my mind wanders at Mass, I am grateful for the sudden movements of the congregation as everyone stands to pray or kneels in adoration of Jesus in the Eucharist. The physical engagement pulls my thoughts away from distractions and back to whatever is happening in the liturgy.

Don't forget that human beings are a unity of body and soul. The movements of our bodies, along with all five senses, can and should be engaged during worship. If you are unable, physically, to join in with the movements of the congregation, it might help to simply adjust your posture with each shift and express more of your intentions with your hands. Whatever mobility you have is part of your connection with God, so find a way to engage your body in worship.

My mind often wanders through the rosary, so I do the obvious: I ask Our Lady to help me to pray! Her beloved Spouse is the Holy Spirit, so I figure she can pull a few strings and call in some added inspiration. Come, Holy Spirit!

Timing is important. If I haven't prayed a rosary by the time I go to bed at night, I very often fall asleep before I finish. So I'll pray a decade each time I drive somewhere or take time while I'm waiting for my daughter at an activity to pray a little more. I might also use the Divine Office app on my smartphone to join the universal Church in praying the Liturgy of the Hours.

I chat with God during physical activities like driving, exercising, folding laundry, or sweeping. Giving him my work, thanking him for his presence, and trying to listen for his promptings enriches my vocation to care for my family and my home. Cultivating an awareness of his presence throughout the day pays major dividends during times of distraction, since it then takes less effort to draw back into the awareness that I've been practicing.

I love the Lighthouse CD of the Month Club. For just a few dollars, the monthly selection comes directly to my mailbox, and I can listen to it at home or in my car to learn more about the rich life of faith and morals of the Catholic Church. The offerings, which feature top Catholic authors and ministry leaders, are entertaining, encouraging, and rich in variety. I consider my subscription a worthwhile investment in a healthy, stimulated brain, as well as an important part of my walk with God.

Inspiring music, art, dance, theater, film, books, and so on, can be a great help. God speaks through the beauty of the arts. Think about what lifts your heart and find a way to integrate it into your life with more consistency. A classical music station, a CD you love, an art print framed on your wall—anything beautiful can be spiritually uplifting, for God is the source and summit of beauty.

The loveliness of the natural world is a powerful reminder of God's presence, giving clues to his conversation with our souls. Simple things like rain pattering on a skylight, sunbeams streaming in a window, or a quiet walk around the neighborhood or a local park can open my heart to God and encourage feelings of gratitude. Even catching sight of a bit of green sprouting up through a sidewalk or a wildflower peeking through stray trash in a vacant lot can remind me of God's grace in the midst of suffering. He's all around us, speaking to us, if we look for him.

Grace at meals is a wonderful sacramental that reminds me to be thankful for the many gifts of my life. The habit of bowing my head to pray, at home or in public, reminds me of the bounty of God's love and his tender care for all my needs. If I find myself rattling off the prayer without connecting it to my heart, I slow down and consider each word, smiling at my Lord in the privacy of my heart.

Pat Gohn, who wrote the foreword for this book, once mentioned that she lights candles at mealtimes to remind her family that Jesus is in their midst. In my home, it has long been our nightly ritual to light candles at the dinner table, whether we are having take-out, leftovers, or a more formal meal. Family time is so precious, and candlelight creates a beautiful, soothing atmosphere for conversation and enjoyment of good food. I consider sharing food to be sacred, since Jesus so loved to feed others, and it is a joy to incorporate a prayer of thanks as the candles are lit, praising God for his presence in our home.

I've been praying with my treasured friend, Annette, a few nights a week, and it has helped us both. Sharing our prayer time has brought more intentionality, focus, and reverence to our meditations on the mysteries of the rosary. We cling to Christ's promise: "Again I say to you, if two of you agree on earth about anything they ask, it will be done for them by my Father in heaven. For where two or three are gathered together in my name, there am I in the midst of them" (Matthew 18:19–20).

I sometimes remember to take a few moments for an end-of-day examination of conscience, and I am trying to make it a nightly habit. *How did I do today? Was I charitable, patient, forgiving? Did I waste time or did I treat each hour as a valuable resource? Was I generous in my responses to demands on my time, or did I avoid responding to the needs of others? Did I step out of the pressures of my life to pray? How can I do better tomorrow?* A quick reflection can help me to focus my prayers and resolutions for the coming day and is a reminder of my great need for God's help in all things.

I forgive myself for the barren days when I fail to pray much at all, the days that fly past in a blur. Each day gets a fresh start with no recriminations. God is merciful, so I try to practice mercy with myself. Kindness given to myself spills over into a greater gentleness and forgiveness toward others.

I don't do all of these things every day, but you get the idea. Whatever helps you to keep moving forward in the spiritual life, keep at it and enjoy it. Change it up, now and then, but persevere without worrying that you're not doing enough or not doing it "right." And don't set unreasonable standards for yourself. It will only lead to disappointment and discouragement. "Let not your hearts be troubled" (John 14:1). God blesses every act of humble trust.

A mature faith can be a great comfort. If my concentration is less than ideal, I might just smile up at God and thank him for his patience, rather than succumb to a fit of self-flagellation. God is perfect, we know; but we never have been perfect and will not ever be perfect, until God purifies our souls himself.

Accepting ourselves is not the same as giving in to or condoning sin. We should work with great commitment to amend our lives, root out our habitual sins, and grow in virtue. By leaning into God's love for us, our souls receive a supernatural boost that reverberates through our lives, into the lives of others, and into eternity.

Chapter Four

WITNESS AND WISDOM
How Our Spiritual Lives Bless Others

She will come to meet him like a mother,
   and like the wife of his youth she will welcome him.
She will feed him with the bread of understanding,
   and give him the water of wisdom to drink.

—Sirach 15:2–3

A soul in love with God is very attractive to other souls. The most ordinary habits of prayer and sacramental life make us potent instruments in the hands of God for touching the hearts and minds of others.

Robyn's Martyr Stories

A friend and colleague of mine, Robyn Lee, has been teaching confirmation classes for many years at her parish in Connecticut. Each year she begins in anxiety, concerned that the distracted teens who have no choice but to sit in her classroom will be bored with her presentation of the Catholic faith. Since her parish program only meets once per month, the pressure to prepare an impactful lesson is pretty intense.

That's why Robyn calls on the saints for help. She has her favorites, many of them martyrs, and she has been learning about them and praying to them for many years. Consequently, she views these saints as much more than just role models; she loves them and considers them friends. She knows their stories in great detail, so she can bring them vividly to life for others. And she realizes that teens need a faith that makes life worth living, but they also need something worth *dying* for. So, at the end of every lesson, Robyn shares a martyr story.

Her love of the martyrs is so passionate that her detailed and dramatic descriptions very nearly become live theater. When she talks about St. Maximilian Kolbe's willingness to die at Auschwitz so that a young father will survive to see his family again, she paces in front of her seated students, her eyes serious. As if the students are the line of prisoners waiting to find out who will live and who will be cast into the starvation pit, she points at them one by one, taking the role of the Nazi guard, and saying, "Will it be you? Or *you*?" They are on the edges of their seats as she describes Kolbe stepping forward to take the young man's place, risking being shot on the spot, and then miraculously surviving for weeks without food or water as he hears confessions in the pit, helping the other victims to die in peace and grace.

She tells the story of St. Maria Goretti, who died from multiple stab wounds as a result of a failed rape attempt, and shows them the stunning love and courage of a young girl. She asks them to explain why, as Maria was being brutally attacked, she cried out, "*No*, Alessandro, it is a *sin!*" At first, they don't understand, so Robyn asks her students, "Is being *raped* a sin? Was she trying to protect herself from God's punishment?" They all shake their heads in the negative. "No, you're right; it's not a sin to be raped," she says. "Maria was worried about *him*. *While he was attacking her,* she was trying to *save his soul!*" The class is transfixed as they consider the incredible guts and faith of this young girl, fighting to save a soul in a terrifying situation.

Robyn's spiritual life spills over into these stories, elevating mere storytelling to a prayerful and courageous act of evangelization. Because the saints are real to her, they become real to her students. They are able to grasp something of God's grace that they have, perhaps, never considered before. This ability to capture their imaginations is not simply a personal talent. This power to plunge a classroom full of teenagers into the drama of divine love is the fruit of a life lived for Christ, soaked in prayer, and abandoned to grace.

A "Language of Love," Just for You

You and I can be powerful evangelists, too. While not everyone is called to the role of a catechist, our Christian vocation is all about sharing the wealth of our spiritual inheritance.

Many years ago, I conducted dozens of interviews with women and men whose talks and writings had inspired me and helped to deepen my relationship with Christ. In this process, I saw myself as sitting at the feet of esteemed spiritual leaders. The main question I asked all of them was, "How do you prepare yourself to hear the voice of God in your life?"

I got a variety of answers, but I noticed a remarkable pattern. Men seemed to sense the movement and guidance of God primarily in retrospect. They could look back over their lives and see the lost job, the amazing opportunity, the injury, or the chance encounter as an essential piece of God's plan to lead them to their true vocation. Important decisions were often carefully made, with much prayer and even consultation with spiritual directors. But ultimately, God's will was not especially clear to them until some time had passed, and they were able to evaluate the *fruits* of their choices.

Women, on the other hand, generally felt God's presence in their everyday lives and could more often sense what God was communicating to them from day to day. In chapter two, I talked about the feminine gift of receptivity. Our openness to receiving the guidance of the Holy Spirit in our lives can be a great strength. When we practice the habit of daily prayer, over time we gradually become more and more certain of the moments when God is giving us a specific word to act on; he speaks to us and we learn to recognize the voice of our humble Shepherd (see John 10:27). The reason for this clarity is that God has devised a "language of love" for each of us that is as individual as we are.

I interviewed Dr. Peter Kreeft[38] about this amazing spiritual individuality. He agreed, saying, "God is like a really great pitcher to kids. He knows how to pitch the ball just right, so every batter is able to hit it." What a delightful image of our tender Lord, carefully crafting messages of guidance, love, and mercy, and sending them home to our hearts in ways that help each of us make contact with the divine.

Over time, the distinctive way God communicates to each of our hearts becomes the language of love that we are invited to enter into and nurture—a special relationship like no other. The hallmarks and identifying quirks of this tender communication system become signposts to identifying the guidance of the Holy Spirit in our lives, like a blazed trail that leads to hidden treasure or a ball pitched just perfectly. The guidance of the Holy Spirit helps us to grow in holiness and virtue, especially wisdom.

Wisdom and "the Woman" in Scripture

Not to brag about women, but it's no accident that femininity is traditionally associated with great virtue, or that virtue is likewise associated with great beauty. In the most influential civilizations of antiquity, the virtue of wisdom was personified as a courageous and beautiful woman.

In ancient Greece, the brave and brilliant archer-goddess, Athena, was worshipped for her wisdom, purity, and heart-slaying good looks, while the Romans called their stunning, warrior-sage-goddess Minerva. Stories abound in mythology of both human and divine males seeking to conquer these illusive women with acts of love and valor.

Scripture does something similar! In the Old Testament's book of Wisdom, wisdom takes the form of a desirable woman sought after and treasured, in this case by King Solomon:

Her I loved and sought after from my youth;
I sought to take her for my bride and was enamored of her
beauty.
She adds to nobility the splendor of companionship with God;
even the Ruler of all loved her.
For she leads into the understanding of God,
and chooses his works.
If riches are desirable in life,
what is richer than Wisdom, who produces all things?
(Wisdom 8:2–5)

Read through the book of Wisdom at your leisure. In particular, take some time to prayerfully read 6:22—8:18. The lovely woman of this meditation is called "intelligent, holy, unique" (Wisdom 7:22), "because of her pureness she pervades and penetrates all things. / For she is a breath of the power of God" (Wisdom 7:24–25).

"The woman" appears elsewhere in Scripture, as an archetype of the Blessed Virgin Mary, whom we call, among her many titles, "Seat of Wisdom." For instance, after the fall of Adam and Eve, God rebukes the serpent who tempted them into disobedience by promising that, through "the woman," the devil will one day be destroyed: "I will put enmity between you and the woman, / and between your seed and her seed; / he shall bruise your head, / and you shall bruise his heel" (Genesis 3:15). The heel, as we know, can sustain injury without bringing death to the body; but God foreshadows the coming of the Messiah when he promises that the offspring of "the woman" will strike a fatal blow to the serpent's head.

In Revelation, St. John's visions reveal a remarkable drama between the "dragon" and "the woman," whom he chases into the desert, bent on destruction:

He pursued the woman who had borne the male child. But the woman was given the two wings of the great eagle that she might fly from the serpent into the wilderness.... The earth came to the help of the woman, and the earth opened its mouth and swallowed the river which the dragon had poured from his mouth. (Revelation 12:13–14, 16)

Incredible imagery. These visions are filled with insight into the spiritual battle waged between the devil and the Blessed Mother. But it is also true that all women, through their gifts of spiritual and/or physical maternity, bring Christ into the world and are given the "wings of the great eagle," God's mighty assistance, to help crush the serpent's head. By relying on God, we grow in holiness and wisdom. By growing in wisdom, we flee to "the wilderness," where we dwell in the protective precincts of our loving God.

Spiritual Motherhood: A Great Marketing Scheme

As I interviewed women for this book, it was a delight to listen to the lovely and intuitive ways women bring their gifts of sensitivity, receptivity, generosity, and maternity to the spiritual life. Women sense God's gentle presence, open their hearts to receive him, ponder the meaning of his promptings, and then generously pour out their maternal hearts to others. By doing so, we invite others to flee with us into God's holy and healing love, and a fascinating dynamic emerges.

Sharing our insights with others often provokes a response, so that through the exchange that results, an idea that may have come to us as a faint whisper in prayer starts to take flesh and grow stronger and clearer within us. Simply put, what we share increases as it is reflected back to us.

Maybe you feel this way: When God seems to tap me on the shoulder and *zap* me with a really good nugget of wisdom, I can't wait to share it.

It feels good to have something valuable to pour out to others, something beautiful with which to nurture and encourage them. And I love the conversations that result. They often surprise me and reveal a facet of God's message to my soul that I would not have considered on my own. It's part of the reason I love to blog.[39]

In recent years, there has been an amazing proliferation of weblogs (aka "blogs," or online journals) about spirituality, motherhood, marriage and family life, health, education, beauty, and a host of other topics interesting to women. They can be fascinating windows into the lives and learning of other women and often provide opportunities for stimulating online discussions. The comments are often as interesting as the posts themselves.

One busy Advent morning, I was imploring God to help me find a spiritual connection to the Nativity in the midst of all the noise and pressure of the season. As I prayed, I was suddenly quite taken with a vivid image of myself reaching for the infant Jesus in the manger, lifting him up to my heart, and cradling him against me. The thought filled me with a vivid sensory connection, which led to a flood of tender affection for baby Jesus. I knew, at that moment, that it would become my Advent meditation.

Soon afterward, I spontaneously shared this insight online, and the post was unusually popular. After a few days of wonderful responses that helped me to treasure the meditation even more, a friend confided in a heartfelt private message that she had been struggling as I had. She was so touched by the idea that it had become her daily meditation, too. The experience felt like so many gifts of grace: Its beauty was multiplied the more I gave it away.

I recently heard Pat Gohn speak about spiritual motherhood at a women's event in New York. She polled the audience, asking how many were biological mothers, adoptive or foster mothers, grandmothers, godmothers, and so on. Hands went up and down. Then she asked, "Any office mothers here? You're the ones that everyone comes to when they're looking for sympathy or Advil." A hearty laugh of recognition rose from the crowd, and a number of women enthusiastically raised their hands, their heads nodding.

No matter what our vocations, talents, or circumstances are, our maternity is likely to be a gift to others. Some forms of spiritual maternity are very deep and complex, as with women who are trained to offer spiritual direction to others. But even for the rest of us, listening more than we speak can be a great gift to those around us. With the hours of our days already stretched thin, it can be a grace-filled gift of love for us to sacrifice a little time for a person in need.

Many ordinary acts of spiritual motherhood can fit easily into our most hectic days: slowing to let another driver into traffic; picking up a dropped item and handing it back to a harried shopper; smiling at the struggling mother of a cranky baby and telling her you "remember it well" and that "it gets better!" Once, I was on the highway and a sports car passed me at high speed, swerving in and out of traffic in a very dangerous fashion. I was seized with the urge to pray for the unseen driver, whom I will probably never meet in this life, but who—I realized with a sense of awe—was personally known and loved by God. Through the gift of even a fleeting spiritual connection, we affirm the immense value and dignity of other human beings.

Here's a thought: If we add to our prayer lists all the people we meet in the course of our days (as a general category), who knows what a difference we may make in their lives? Perhaps, when we finally enter heaven, a huge army of people who were touched by God's grace through some simple gesture or act of kindness of ours, including our faithful prayers, will be waiting to welcome us home with great joy. What a privilege to be messengers of love in a thousand small ways and know that, while the rest of the world may overlook these gestures, Almighty God honors our efforts and lends them his power.

Wisdom in Times of Suffering

Jesus urges us to take up our crosses and follow him (see Matthew 16:24), so we know that there is value in our suffering. Through even the most hesitant attempt at joining our sufferings to the cross of Christ, God's generosity is unleashed into our souls and brings healing and wisdom.

A dear friend of mine is suffering from the devastating effects of her post-chemo medication. Jane has been fighting for her life for so long that she has lost her grip on "ordinary." Every day seems to bring another shock, another challenge, another loss. If it were my suffering, I'd be resentful. But she's not. She radiates a childlike simplicity and a humility so lovely that her eyes have been transformed. No longer merely intelligent, they are clear and luminous, as if heaven were shining through them.

On January 19, 2013, Jane knelt in the quiet of her parish church after Mass, praying. As the focus of her Advent observance, she had spiritually adopted her beloved brother, Bill, a brilliant Harvard Ph.D.—and an atheist. After Christmas, she was disappointed in herself. She hadn't done much that would make a worthy offering for her brother.

That morning, as she prayed, she thought she heard her Lord ask her a question: *Would you sacrifice your life to save your brother's soul?*

"You've got the wrong person," she protested immediately. "I'm not brave at all. I don't have it in me to do that." She caught her breath. "But whatever you want. You're *God.*"

The next day, Jane detected a large, ominous lump in her breast.

In short order, a diagnosis of stage-three breast cancer sent this all-natural, drug-free mom into major surgery and several rounds of chemotherapy and radiation. Of course, the process was devastating, and because her cancer was advanced, her treatments were followed up with highly toxic anti-tumor drugs. As a result, her once sparkling, nuanced thought processes were reduced to a slow-motion struggle to cope with ordinary tasks.

"I'd be cooking dinner, staring at the broccoli, thinking, 'Maybe...I should...get a knife to cut it.' Everything was in slow motion," she remembers. She was prohibited from driving, and her already hard-working husband had to take up the slack in a thousand ways, leaving him stressed and exhausted. Her doctors didn't know why she was having symptoms that looked an awful lot like Alzheimer's.

After several months and much prayer, Jane walked into church one morning, and as she passed the tabernacle, the strong and certain thought came to her that her anti-tumor medicine was causing neuro-toxicity in her brain. She stopped taking the drugs that night and has gradually come back to herself, though the specter of tumor growth makes her decision a risky one.

Looking back on the period during which her greatest pride, her ability to *think*, was stripped away, she expresses a reluctant appreciation for the immensity of the suffering she experienced, because it brought her a new vision of herself and brought about a radical shift in her relationships: "What has happened in recent months has been an exercise in humility. Last Lent, I was drawn to live the Scripture, 'I am among you as one who serves' (Luke 22:27), even when I was going through a total cognitive meltdown."

According to Jane, she was a product of "law school feminism," which held as one of its commandments, "Don't ever do anything for anyone over five that they can do for themselves." To bend to serve her family would be "door-mattish," she had always thought. Even before she was sick, her husband, also an attorney, was tasked each weekday with getting the children's breakfast, packing their lunches, and getting everyone off to school, all before he left for work.

After all, she'd never been a morning person. "6:20 A.M. was like the middle of the night to me," she says, laughing. So Mike did all the morning chores, and Jane woke up hours later to do whatever she wanted. It seemed fair, at the time.

Then, in the midst of her cognitive struggles, pressed down by the debilitating effects of her medication and stripped of any intellectual pride, she had a life-changing epiphany. "All of a sudden, it dawned on me that it wasn't fair!" she says in amazement. She started setting her alarm and taking care of all the morning chores, even making her husband's lunch so that he could get to the gym before work each day.

Jane was amazed at the change in herself and the happiness that it gave her family. "I thought I'd be resentful, but rather than feeling that way, it makes me feel more love for them," she says with great feeling. "By the time I go to the 8:30 Mass, I've already given love to all these people!"

When asked about offering her sufferings to God, she told me the story of St. Faustina having a vision of Jesus in which he showed her three people: one dragging the cross, one carrying it, and one nailed to it in complete surrender. Jesus said to her, "How much value is there in each?"

"Obviously," says Jane, "the totally surrendered one is the most valuable, but I am definitely in the dragging, muttering, worrying, complaining group. And I know that takes away the spiritual power of it; I try to remind myself of that. But the great grace of suffering is that it puts this *enormous power* in your life; and if you embrace it, you can make a difference in the salvation of the world—and, of course, your own salvation."

It's stirring to know someone of such humility, throwing her life into God's hands in the midst of the worst suffering. I liken it, in a strange way, to adventure heroes in literature and in films, who find themselves in the worst possible predicaments. They are hemmed in on all sides, their backs against some unscalable wall; they are outnumbered and out-gunned, and death seems certain. But suddenly they see a chink in that formidable wall, and what was once an obstacle becomes a pathway to joy. They reach up to grasp the newly discovered handhold, hauling themselves upward to safety.

Grace is like that chink in the wall, because through God's power we can open to blessings that transcend the ordinary. He comes to us and gives us exactly what we need, when we need it, if we do our best to trust him.

Time Shifts

Many women reinvent themselves in the second half of their lives, opening businesses, traveling to far off places, learning to paint, reconnecting with old friends, pursuing long-held dreams. It can be a time of adventure and thrilling exploration.

Yet it can be painful and confusing, just as we are on the verge of realizing cherished plans, to accept with grace new burdens that sometimes arrive on our doorsteps unannounced: upheaval in our religious order; a divorced adult child in need of a place to live; a grandchild who needs to enroll in Granny's special daycare; a chronically ill spouse or aging parent whose health issues threaten to make us housebound, too.

Some women are forced back into the stressful world of time clocks and deadlines because of a financial disaster or an ailing loved one.

Many, once highly qualified, stepped out of the career track long ago to raise families. They haven't kept up with their professions because they were looking forward to "the volunteer years" of retirement, only to be confronted with their husbands' underemployment and their children's college tuitions. Up in smoke go all their lovely plans, as they gear back up to enter the workforce.

Whatever the issues, our lives can suddenly assume a shape and a pace we hadn't anticipated. When this happens, it can seem that we die a little as we detach from our expectations. But, like the most beautiful Christian paradoxes, the mortification of our own desires can lead to more life and more blessings than we ever thought possible.

Acceptance and Grace

There's nothing so ennobling as the determination to carry our crosses in a spirit of love and hope. Willing acceptance unleashes spiritual treasures that pour into our souls with great power, turning our expectations inside out and bringing light to the darkness of our hearts.

It's been true, so often in my life, that at the moment when I am most likely to sink into self-pity or resentment, if I manage to turn my heart to God, my small act of faith bears fruit immediately. If the moment of suffering calls for forgiveness and I cooperate with God's grace, I see how my relationships open up in new ways. Or, if God is calling me to repentance and I humble myself to make amends and seek sacramental reconciliation, I experience healing in my own life and the lives of those around me.

So often I have confessed a sin, only to have another part of my life healed that I didn't know had any connection to that sin. Repentance of impure thoughts and acts visibly opens our relationships to greater trust and love, while sorrow for dishonesty seems to link directly to an increase in generosity within the family. I suspect that absolution drives out fear and, amidst the shower of sacramental graces, liberates us, step by mysterious step.

There are so many of these special moments of grace. Each time we die to self, we uncover the hidden beauty of the cross. Putting others first is Christ's surprising, powerful way to peace and joy. Sacrifice is the unexpected key to the treasure; it opens our sinful nature to the stunning, life-giving forces of God's self-donating love.

In fact, there is no better antidote to spiritual dryness than to make an act of selfless love. The Church has always called us to serve the poor and suffering around us, especially within our own homes. It helps to contemplate the spiritual and corporal works of mercy and do our best to practice them.

The Corporal Works of Mercy:
- Feed the hungry
- Give drink to the thirsty
- Clothe the naked
- Shelter the homeless
- Visit the sick
- Visit the imprisoned
- Bury the dead

The Spiritual Works of Mercy:
- Admonish the sinner
- Instruct the ignorant
- Counsel the doubtful
- Comfort the sorrowful
- Bear wrongs patiently
- Forgive all injuries
- Pray for the living and the dead

Thanks to technology, even those who are homebound are able to use their phones or computers to send donations to worthy charities or flowers to the bereaved, counsel the doubtful and sorrowful, or feed the hunger of lonely people by listening, loving, and interceding. We would all benefit from praying for the living and the dead, and we can ask God for the grace to forgive those who have wounded us. Any of these little offerings can do so much good and jumpstart our joy.

In fact, every moment spent in prayer increases the treasury of grace on earth for souls! We serve simply by humbling ourselves before God. There are countless ways to serve and, therefore, just as many ways to rediscover the delights of the spiritual life. Sometimes we feel there isn't enough love in our hearts to serve wholeheartedly. It helps to consider the "Little Way" of St. Thérèse.

The Little Way of the Smile

It comforts me enormously that St. Thérèse of Lisieux (aka "the Little Flower") never let any of her human weaknesses frighten her away from intimacy with God. Her "Little Way" was full of audacious confidence in his mercy:

> Yes, I feel it; even though I had on my conscience all the sins that can be committed, I would go, my heart broken with sorrow, and throw myself into Jesus' arms, for I know how much He loves the prodigal child who returns to Him.[40]

Thérèse believed she was too small and weak to achieve holiness, but she trusted Jesus to tenderly lift her to sanctity: "The elevator which must raise me to heaven is Your arms, O Jesus! And for this I had no need to grow up, but rather I had to remain *little* and become this more and more."[41]

All her observations on the spiritual life are like that: brimming with the joyful expectation that God is good and kind, worthy of our trust, and eager to help us. Eventually, she was named a saint and doctor of the Church! The key, she makes clear, is to abandon ourselves to Jesus, to be humble enough to accept that without him we are nothing at all; but with him, we can do anything (see Philippians 4:13).

It makes sense, doesn't it? Jesus lowered himself, becoming a poor human infant, and then lived as an ordinary carpenter for many years before beginning his public ministry. He often spent many hours in prayer, sometimes throughout the night, asking for everything he needed to conduct his ministry. The Father responded by sending him apostles, signs, and miracles that stunned the world. If the divine Son embraced dependence and humility, who are we to do otherwise?

So many of the women I have interviewed for this book possess a similar confidence in God and happily associate it with maturity. Having lived and loved through the hectic and complicated early decades of their vocations, careers, and families, it seems to be a natural progression after midlife for women to simplify their prayer lives and to cultivate a companionable awareness of God in their midst, from moment to moment, each day.

They have learned that God hears their prayers in an effortless and uncomplicated way. They know that they don't have to be flawless spiritual beings to be loved and treasured by God. They profit from spiritual victories as they learn to move out of God's way and cooperate with his grace—even when his will is at odds with their own. They become, like the Little Flower, capable of resting in confidence and trust. This simplicity may seem counterintuitive in the context of maturity, but laying claim to our littleness and dependency on God makes women formidable in the spiritual life.

Chapter Five

ONE IS SILVER AND THE OTHER GOLD
Friendships That Last

Let love be genuine; hate what is evil, hold fast to what is
good; love one another with brotherly affection; outdo one
another in showing honor.

—Romans 12:9–10

Most of us have heard the old adage, "Beauty is only skin deep." The
original expression, drawn from a poem by the seventeenth-century
poet Sir Thomas Overbury, actually read, "All the carnall *beauty* of my
wife, is but skin deep"[42] and was part of a lengthy description of the
perfect wife. Full of dire warnings against immoral women who wield
the power of lust to control foolish men, the poet urged his reader
to look deeper, to value the true beauty one finds only in a virtuous
woman. Sadly, much of our culture is programmed by our mass media
to think of beauty as actually *being* skin deep. Fad diets, cosmetic
surgeries, and even corsets have become big business, even among the
young, as desperate women reject their own natural loveliness in favor
of a punishing devotion to a false ideal.

Who Is Beautiful to You?

Allow me to ask you a question: Which women exemplify beauty in
your life? Put this book down and let your mind roam a little until you
are clear about what you really think. When you're done, read on, and
I'll tell you what happened when I asked myself the same question.

For me, the first images I thought of were stock photos—nothing very original. Maybe you saw these, too. Supermodels appeared in my mind, tawny and suntanned, perfectly toned with glossy hair and full lips, swathed in body-hugging fashions. Second, a parade of movie stars flitted through, like the next wave on a fashion runway. But as they were appearing, my mind was already pushing them aside, searching through a cacophony of canned answers for something real and personal. For a vulnerable moment, I worried that no other images would arise—that maybe I didn't know what I thought apart from my cultural programming.

In the next instant, several women I have known over the years came to mind, one by one, each of them lovely in different ways. I had to laugh at the way I categorized them—principally by the color of their hair: the athletic brunette; the shy, bookish redhead; the smart granola blonde; the impish, white-haired nonagenarian. I noted a certain comfort in their own bodies and each woman's pleasure in some aspect of her femininity, a sort of glamour unique to each.

In a rush, I felt again the warmth of easy smiles and gentle spirits, and it occurred to me that, while each of these women was also good looking, the genuine qualities of beauty that I could readily and sincerely identify were mostly aspects of character or emotional well-being. Each possessed a trait that I admired, even envied a little, and had tried to emulate. Ultimately, I realized that my feelings of delight in each of these beautiful women were more about how they made me feel about myself than their actual physical beauty; more about the way their friendship or acts of kindness inspired me to be a better person in some way; more about the ways that spending time in their company had led me to reevaluate my own expressions of femininity.

Try something right now. Make a quick tally of the women who represent some aspect of beauty to you. Don't think about it too much at first; just list them. Once you have their names or descriptions—since we are sometimes affected by strangers—take note of what makes each woman beautiful to you. Here are a few thoughts to get you started:

Is she passionate and joyful in her vocation?

Is she elegantly pulled together or brimming with healthy vitality?

Does she make you laugh or, even better, love your jokes?

Does she listen when you need an ear, share her hard-won wisdom when you ask for it, make a great cup of coffee, or see the best in you when you have trouble seeing it yourself?

Were there any surprises or difficulties? Does the culture's obsession with false perfection make the notion of beauty confusing or painful for you? Are there ways you can express a greater appreciation for the price-less attributes of the women you value in your life? Are there ways that this appreciation might help to heal your own wounded femininity?

Once you have taken time to respond, consider sharing this exercise with a trusted friend. If you do, listen without judgment, staying open to her no matter what. She has had her own family or ethnic culture to consider, as well as a lifetime of personal experiences and relationships. If you are open, you'll discover so much about each other's values, as well as areas where each of you needs support.

Our Need for Friendship

We all need companionship—it's the way God made us. But even as mature women, we don't always know how to find good friends, or even how to keep the ones we have. Our lives are demanding, and we haven't always had the time, energy, or opportunity to cultivate close relation-ships beyond our vocations, careers, and marriages. In the second half of our lives, a time when so many women rediscover or reinvent them-selves, it's a good idea to discern thoughtfully what actually constitutes a worthy relationship and what it takes to be a good friend to another woman.

I recently stumbled upon some terrific guidelines for healthy relationships in an unexpected place: an online translation of a document written by the legendary second-century Roman statesman, Cicero.[43] It seems odd to find something of value for contemporary, Christian women in the writings of an ancient, pagan man, but his relationship advice is so much better than a lot of what passes for wisdom in women's magazines. The trend in society is to be all about selfish fulfillment and transitory pleasures, but I was happy to discover that many of Cicero's points meshed nicely with solid Christian values. Wisdom is wisdom and truth is truth, no matter who the bearer is. I'll summarize his points and add some thoughts from my own life, the writings of the saints, and the Church.

His first point was that friendship is supposed to lift us up and help us to be better people, not worse ones, so our bonds of love should never be used to compel another person to commit a moral wrong. If my friend asks me to do something that makes me uncomfortable, I need to have the strength to say no, even if I am entreated on the basis of love or loyalty. Likewise, if I am tempted to put my friend on the spot to cover up my mistakes, avoid responsibility, or help me cheat the system in some way—perhaps by stopping in to the retail establishment where she works and implicitly pressuring her to share her employee discount—then I'm not being a true friend to her. Again, friends should want what is best for each other, never seeking to use or manipulate each other into sinful acts for their own selfish benefit.

Second, the best friendships occur between virtuous people. Like attracts like, so if I want to appeal to the best possible companions, I have to work on growing in virtue. It's a strange thing, but we can spot each other, instinctually. We tend to be drawn to people who are roughly at our own level of character development, or to those on a similar trajectory who may have something to teach us. What we possess ourselves, even to a limited degree, we become capable of recognizing and valuing in others.

Third, Cicero advised looking for the best in others, focusing on the personality traits and habits of our friends that are noble, beautiful, and admirable—whether or not our friends are flawless models of rectitude. St. Thérèse of Lisieux believed that the best parts of a person are the most true parts, since they are of God. Think about that for a moment. The deficits in human character are of less importance than what is good, true, and beautiful. Anything ennobling is connected directly to the divine, so when we allow ourselves to be edified by whatever goodness we can perceive in another person, we ourselves draw closer to God.

I can't tell you how many times this notion of emphasizing and honoring goodness has saved me from falling headlong into judgmental assumptions about the people closest to me. Such condemnation is unjust, to be sure, since I am certainly not an incorrupt or omnipotent judge; and indulging my appetite for critiquing others would have diverted attention from my own faults (see Matthew 7:1–5) and made a scapegoat of someone else's. It's a dangerous trap to habitually take note of other people's failings, and it can stop our own spiritual growth in its tracks.

I need to pay close attention to my own failings so I can confess them and be healed, rather than wasting precious time griping about someone else's sins, no matter how valid the complaint might be. In fact, focusing on what's best in people quickly becomes a pleasure, and the more we direct our attention to what is good and beautiful, the more grace lifts up our relationships. Forgiveness and mercy are incredibly liberating to both the forgiver and the forgiven.

Finally, Cicero pointed out that to focus on each other's faults is to file away complaints for the inevitable breakdown of the relationship. It's like pretending to be friends while planning for the day when we will be enemies. Instead of providing opportunities to practice charity, patience, and forgiveness, the laundry list of faults becomes ammunition stored up for the war to come. Let's face it, odds are that both we and our friends have many faults, and the closer we get to one another, the clearer those faults appear to us. If we're going to stay in relationship, we need to chill out and give other people a break.

There may be exceptions to this proposed rule of forbearance, as when we suffer a deliberate act of betrayal that would indicate a serious breakdown in trust. The gossipy companion who thinks nothing of character assassination might be someone to avoid, for instance. Only you can decide where to draw the line.

However, as a rule, we must decide if we are looking for excuses to dump our friends to avoid amending our own lives, or if we're really in these relationships to witness to the sacrificial love of Jesus Christ: to help our friends into heaven, lighten their burdens, and honor their inherent value as children of God.

True Friendship Is a Glimpse of Heaven

For the first time in many years, I have a best friend outside the ranks of my extended family, and I treasure Annette for the gift she truly is. She's about eleven years younger than I am, but because I was nearly forty when I became a mother, we are in a similar season with our children. In the last few years, our almost daily contact through texts, calls, or e-mails has become an essential touchstone in my life, bringing a special kind of connectedness and joy. When we're together, the intersection of our busy, homeschooling lives is a work of art in progress, continuing to unfold with a complementary dynamism that still surprises me and makes me feel blessed to have a certain "standing" in this delightful person's life.

I recently read Lisa Hendey's superb book *The Grace of Yes: Eight Virtues for Generous Living*, and was brought up short by something she wrote in the second chapter. Commenting on the tendency to appreciate her best friends for the qualities they possess and their ability to strengthen and complete her in areas where she feels she is lacking, she casts a wary eye: "Instead of standing in awe of the friends I named above for the simple fact that they are of God, his beautiful creations and an image of his divine love, I err by reflecting on our relationships as through a mirror, aimed squarely at my own ego."[44]

Lisa's insight really made me stop and think. Do I value my friends for who they are, for their value as human persons made in the image and likeness of God, or for what they give me? Do I rely on my BFFs to make me feel good? To remind me that I am valued? To provide a place to vent, to confide and cry, to share prayer intentions, funny stories, adventures, or a cup of tea? Well, yes. Yes to all of those things.

Yet, pondering the inherent worth of my friends helps me to treasure them all the more and with slightly less self-interest. Each of my friends has a purpose, a dignity that is a gift—not just to me, but to the divine plan of salvation for the Church and the world. Each is a glimpse of the Divine Friend, each relationship a foretaste of the joys of heaven to come. Through the various qualities, lessons, and graces that these relationships bring to my life, I experience subtle opportunities to enter into conversation with God. Through their goodness, I experience God's goodness. Through their encouragement, counsel, and fellowship, my life is blessed, and my soul is better prepared to receive God's grace.

The Seasons of Friendship

When I ask women over sixty to talk about the value of their friendships, they describe an interesting progression. Earlier in life, careers, vocations, or children offered situations that promoted enjoyable relationships. During those years, life was intense and friendships were abundant, so the mobility and relative instability of friendships was of little concern. However, for a lucky few, some of those early relationships endured beyond their original context. Over the years, the friendships that survived became increasingly precious, as available options thinned out for a variety of reasons: changes in marital or vocational status, mental or physical incapacitation, retirement migrations, death, or other circumstances that created obstacles to closeness and connection.

When I meet women in their eighties and nineties who still enjoy vibrant social lives, it's heartwarming to listen to them talk about lifelong friendships, as well as new ones. They exhibit a healthy mental toughness that serves their relationships well, a tendency to tolerate each other's foibles with more generosity and good humor than they might have employed in their youth. Being quirky or less than perfect—even quite irritating, in some cases—just isn't a deal breaker if one's connection has survived the rigors of time and experience. This is especially true if friends, even relatively new ones, have seen each other through difficult times.

This peculiar permanence in the face of conflict or chronic annoyances doesn't mean that mature ladies don't complain about each other, mind you. It can be quite entertaining to hear them vent about each other's idiosyncrasies, as with one woman who hilariously described the stinginess of one of her oldest friends. While the lady's financial situation was more than adequate to occasionally purchase a nice dessert, she had taken her turn to host a group of friends for a Bible study and served two stale donuts cut into small pieces as the only refreshment!

Her guests were appalled but too polite to comment. As the story was recounted, the speaker rolled her eyes good-naturedly and said, "That's just *her!*" With so much shared history comes the realization that old comrades are irreplaceable; so if a friend is tight with a buck, bossy, or boring, she's still likely to receive an invitation to the next card party or ladies' night out. Her quirks are just not as critical as her capacity to bear witness to a shared history of joys and sorrows. Walking together through suffering makes sisters of girlfriends and makes valued relationships priceless.

Sometimes this "sisterhood" sneaks up on us. At any time of life, if the changes in one woman's life mirror similar changes in the life of another, their hearts will sometimes open in curiosity and sympathy. Perhaps they are both new to a parish ministry or retirement community, have been invited to sit on the board of a beloved charity, or have discovered a shared interest via social media. The new friend may already be an acquaintance from the woman's wider circle of contacts, with whom she previously lacked a deep connection, but changing circumstances and mutual need sometimes combine to generate an intimacy that would not have been likely before.

In particular, widowhood sometimes opens the door to new relationships, as former caretakers of ailing spouses experience the mixed blessing of a sudden abundance of free time. After the initial shock of losing her beloved life partner gives way and she feels more herself, a widow may wish to pursue interests and activities that were out of reach before her husband's passing, to embrace life again and redefine herself as an individual. If she doesn't fall prey to depression, her loneliness can be a wonderful motivator for reengaging in volunteer work, clubs, and other social opportunities. She will always miss him, but her life, she discovers among friends, is far from over.

The phenomenon of friendships that emerge from shared suffering is so much more than the old cliché, "Misery loves company." It's actually the result of a kind of innate feminine wisdom: the receptivity and generosity of spiritual motherhood that prompts us to console an acquaintance or even a stranger, to speak a language to her that we sense few others can, because they don't know her pain as we do. No one understands the aching void left behind when a husband dies unless they've experienced it themselves, so widows tend to find each other, offering their support and sharing their feelings. Of course, not all of us marry, and we don't only suffer from bereavement.

Knowing that an acquaintance is similarly afflicted, whatever the circumstances, can be an opportunity to bond. Whether she is grieving a loss of health, struggling to accept a diminished involvement in her religious order, missing a cherished career, or longing for an adult child living far from home, the "dark valleys" (see Psalm 23:4) we pass through are fertile ground for intimate connections that can ulti- mately bring great happiness. Intuitively, we know we are not meant to be alone, so we move toward the pain of those who mirror our own. Shared misfortune becomes strength, and that strength brings perspec- tive, which makes way for new life and new hope.

God floods our lives with blessings when we make the selfless choice to minister to others disoriented by loss. Accepting help when we need it can be an opportunity for grace, as well. It takes real courage to move toward a friendship that may shake us out of our sadness and support our healing, just as it takes a holy trust to open our hearts to women who may be carrying heavy loads themselves.

Friendship with the Saints and Holy Souls
The book of Ruth is a very short, but inspiring, four chapters, tucked in the Bible between Judges and 1 Samuel, and recounts the history of one of Jesus Christ's truly remarkable ancestors. A pagan Moabite woman, Ruth married a Jewish man whose family had settled in her homeland

during a time of famine in the land of Judah. She dearly loved her mother-in-law, Naomi, so when both of their husbands died, Ruth adopted the Jewish faith and dedicated all her strength and resourcefulness to protecting Naomi from loneliness and poverty. Leaving her pagan beliefs, her home, and her kin behind, she accompanied Naomi on the long journey back to Judah to try to make a new life.

As a result, God's favor brought blessings that would make Ruth the wife of Naomi's relative, the honorable and influential farmer, Boaz. Ruth's son, Obed, would eventually become the father of Jesse, providing an essential link in the line of King David and leading ultimately to the birth of Christ. With its emphasis on sacrificial love and family ties, the book of Ruth, the commentary tells us, "grips its audience with profound insight into divine and human relationships."[45]

Another story of friendship that is worthy of prayerful study concerns Mary and Elizabeth (see Luke 1:39–45). In the moments following the annunciation, in which the archangel Gabriel asks the young Virgin Mary to become the Mother of the Messiah, he also reveals that Mary's elderly cousin, Elizabeth, is miraculously pregnant. Forgetting herself completely, Mary packs and travels to the hill country, devoting herself to loving and serving Elizabeth in her time of need.

Not for a moment does Mary sit back and gloat, wallowing in the honor of her chosen status. Newly pregnant herself, she leaps at the opportunity to sacrifice her own comforts to help Elizabeth with her household chores. With similar humility, Elizabeth, inspired by the Holy Spirit, exults at the sound of Mary's greeting. She is the first to recognize her little cousin as the "most highly favored" Mother of God's divine Son, as her own son, John the Baptist, leaps for joy in her womb. It is a tender account, full of joy and acceptance of the mysteries of God.

As Catholics, we are blessed with a superabundance of role models for faith and friendship, but saints and biblical heroes are much more than just models to imitate. The Church urges us to engage in living friendships with the saints in heaven, as well as the holy souls in purgatory, just as we do with our family and friends here on earth. This fellowship of souls among the living, those in purgatory, and those in heaven is called "the communion of saints."

The *Catechism of the Catholic Church* tells us, "Exactly as Christian communion among our fellow pilgrims brings us closer to Christ, so our communion with the saints joins us to Christ, from whom as from its fountain and head issues all grace..." (957; see Ephesians 4:1–6). In fact, when we offer our prayers for the souls in purgatory, "Our prayer for them is capable not only of helping them, but also of *making their intercession for us effective*" (*CCC* 958; see 1371, 1032, 1689; emphasis mine). Our friendship with the holy souls becomes "an exchange of spiritual goods," (*CCC* 955) as we intercede for one another.

While the holy souls are being purified in order to enter heaven, their joy and sorrow mingle in anticipation of eternal joy. They are making their final journey into the spectacular light of heaven, and their holiness and intercessory powers are considerable. Friendship with these dear ones—both strangers and loved ones alike—who long for our prayers to help alleviate their suffering, can be a powerful alliance that elicits an outpouring of healing and protective graces to every area of our lives.

Through our Catholic faith, we discover an extraordinary connectedness with what Scripture calls "the heavenly host."[46] I love the image of the "cloud of witnesses" that St. Paul describes in his letter to the Hebrews (see Hebrews 12:1–2). Like a multitude of sports fans watching us play out our lives in the earthly arena, they cheer us on as we do battle with our sins. In fact, they surround us continually, drawing down graces to help us grow in holiness and watching with eyes of love as we fight our way to heaven. In the infinitely loving presence of Almighty God, the members of our heavenly family—the Blessed Mother, the souls in purgatory, angels, and saints—watch over us with great interest and are deeply moved when we call upon them for help.

Many women's lives have been influenced by the intercessory friendship of a particular saint who seemed to come into their lives at exactly the right moment, as a channel of grace and healing. My longtime friend, Juliet, a lovely British lady in her sixties, recently told me that after her husband died, she was inconsolable. Their marriage had been close and tender, and the loss had devastated her. In the depths of despair, she clung to the writings of St. Julian of Norwich, a fourteenth-century mystic, to whom Jesus appeared, saying, "...all shall be well...all manner of things shall be well..." [47] Juliet declared in a recent e-mail, "I hang my hat on those words."

When I was going through my re-conversion to Catholicism back in 1992, I met a woman at a retreat house who loved St. Thérèse of Lisieux. One day at lunch, she seemed to sense a need in me and spontaneously witnessed to the power of the saint's intercession. I was spellbound. I had never met anyone dedicated to studying the life of a particular saint before, and this woman had taken it much further. She had written a master's thesis on Thérèse's life, and in the process, made the Little Flower's spirituality a major feature of her own.

This kind stranger's radiant witness prompted me to purchase a book about Thérèse's life, plunging me into my first important relationship with a Catholic saint. I quickly learned that the most common sign of an intercessory response from St. Thérèse was the appearance of roses. When I returned home from the retreat, two-dozen red roses were waiting in a vase on my kitchen table, a spontaneous gift from my husband. Twenty-three years later, when I stop to think about the beautiful women who are my most treasured friends, I count St. Thérèse, my extraordinary sister in Christ, among them.

Chapter Six

VOWS OF LOVE
Nurturing Our Vocations

Speak, for thy servant hears.

—1 Samuel 3:10

For as long as I can remember, I have wanted to be a mother. The fourth of six children (and the third daughter), I was accustomed to hand-me-downs. So, when I was three and my parents gave me my first brand-new baby doll for Christmas, I was swept away with delight and tenderness for "my baby." I couldn't believe she was really mine, and I cast sidelong looks at my siblings, worried that, at any moment, she might be snatched from my hands.

My mother remembers the stunned reverence with which I cradled my doll and carried her everywhere, soothing her as if she were a real child. The funny thing is, I remember it, too, in vivid detail. I remember the bliss of holding my perfect dolly in the glow of my mother's tender smiles, as she watched me mimic all·the ministrations of motherhood that I had learned from her. There was no one more special to me than my mom, so I had observed her closely.

This radiant moment of shared happiness still lives poignantly in my memory. When I reflect on it as a wife and mom, I can see that it was an early instance of my own conversation with God. The joy of that toddler's Christmas morning would be echoed and greatly amplified more than thirty-six years later, when I first held my newborn daughter, Theresa, after many years of infertility.

This ongoing dialogue with God, which for each of us manifests itself in countless, personal ways over the years, has the power to lead us to our soul's greatest possible fulfillment. Consider this divine message spoken by the prophet, Jeremiah: "Before I formed you in the womb I knew you, / and before you were born I consecrated you" (Jeremiah 1:5). "For I know the plans I have for you...plans for welfare and not for evil, to give you a future and a hope" (Jeremiah 29:11). The real question for each of us is not, *Does God have a specific and beautiful plan for my life?* Instead, we should ask, *Do I appreciate it for the blessing it is?*

Hearing God's Call

Sister Bernarda radiates a quiet joy that makes her lovely face even more attractive. A Polish Missionary Sister of St. Benedict, she works at a Catholic home for the aged and volunteers as a catechist in a nearby parish. She possesses a natural charm and impish sense of humor that makes her popular with both children and adults.

Sister Bernarda remembers the first inkling of her call to religious life, in childhood, when her grandmother lived with the family. A saintly person, her grandmother went about serving the sick and even took in a pregnant teenager at a time when she would have been stigmatized. She kept a small altar in her room, with a beautiful statue of the Blessed Virgin Mary.

From the time she was nine years old, Bernarda was "fascinated with religious life" and made faithful visits to her grandmother's altar in the morning, at midday, and at night. Young Bernarda would run to the altar when no one was looking, say a short prayer before the statue of the Blessed Mother, and then dart away before anyone noticed. Two of her aunts, a cousin, and a niece also became nuns, and her family was devoutly Catholic, so her vocation was accepted and encouraged.

A very special colleague of mine, Louise, lives out her vocation as a consecrated virgin, while she works full-time in publishing. In the late

1980s, when she was in her thirties, she first discerned the call. "I found my vocation when I wasn't really looking for it. I had a strong desire to live my life for God and to do whatever I could to love him more…to make my life something that would build his kingdom. But it was still a surprise to me when I felt he was calling me to a consecrated life."

Some of her friends had already settled on consecrated virginity as the answer to their prayers, but Louise continued to visit religious communities. "Over time, it became more and more clear to me that I was being invited to be a consecrated virgin. God has been kind to me because he impressed this so strongly that I have never doubted that this is his call for me. I may doubt my ability to live it out, but I never doubt that God's grace is there for me."

Tracey, a married mother of five children remembers that it took time for her to see her marriage as a vocation. She sums it up this way: "When you first get married, you're all caught up in the exterior, like the excitement of the wedding and the honeymoon. Then you start to see that things are not so perfect, and you realize you have to stick it out. You have to grow and ask God for help."

The Beauty in Every Vocation

The lifeblood of every vocation is the realization that we are most completely ourselves when we love sacrificially, strengthened by prayer and sacramental life. Living in divine love is the only answer to our human longings. We are made in the image and likeness of God, so it is only by loving as he does that we find fulfillment.

St. Thérèse wrote of her own vocation, "I understood that love embraces all vocations, that it is all things, and that it reaches out through all the ages, and to the uttermost limits of the earth, because it is eternal. Then, beside myself with joy, I cried out: 'O Jesus, my Love…. my *vocation*, at last I have found it…. MY VOCATION IS LOVE!'"[48]

What Thérèse said about love encompassing all vocations thrills my soul. Through love, every vocation finds its essential meaning, vitality, and beauty. Whatever our own vocation may be, it is useful to meditate on some of the different callings that draw women along various holy paths to the same wellspring of fulfillment.

Consecrated virginity, whether in the world or in religious communities, is a spousal relationship, with each woman committing her entire life, with great love, to Jesus Christ as her spiritual husband. Her life's emphasis is on total self-gift in the service of God. The impact of this single-hearted witness cannot be overestimated; in a world bent on self-gratification, the total yielding of one's life to God speaks eloquently of divine love, as well as a deep faith in the supreme happiness of the life to come.

Sister Bernarda says, "The joys of my vocation are prayer and the holy Mass, being with the Lord, and communal life. It is a great joy and a struggle, growing together. We all have different approaches, likes and dislikes. Those differences provide chances to grow. It is painful, but in pain new life is born." She marvels at how attached she is to all the sisters. "When any of the sisters goes on vacation, I can't wait until they come back! Her absence leaves a void. We are like a family."

She remembers that her own mother, a happily married woman, loved to dance. When she was younger, she would attend every village celebration with delight. Later, when Sister Bernarda found joy in her own vocation, she says, "I began to dance with the Lord! Whatever I do, whether I clean, pray, or teach, I ask him to lead. Sometimes I step on the feet of the Lord, so Jesus and I embrace in the sacrament of confession, and the dance of love continues. That is the beauty of it! Jesus said, 'Whoever wants to follow me must renounce himself,' and I find that being obedient to other people gives me joy. Being disobedient makes me unhappy."

As Louise lives out her call to consecrated virginity, she enjoys an extraordinary privilege: With permission from her local bishop, the Blessed Sacrament is kept in a private chapel in her home. Louise can visit with Jesus at any time. My mind reels with the enormity of it. I wonder, *If I had Jesus physically living with me, would it completely change my life?*

Louise says:

> The very heart of being a consecrated virgin is giving every part of yourself in love to Jesus—to have him as your spouse, your first and only love, and your total destiny. Every person is called to love Jesus, but as a consecrated woman, that love permeates every part of my life. All of us are meant to bear fruit for God's kingdom, and God has put me in Catholic publishing where I can bring God's truth to so many thousands of people. That is a great joy to me, but at my deepest heart, my joy is in giving myself to Jesus and knowing that he gives himself to me. This is a love that reflects the very heart of God, and I have been invited to share in it. I can't imagine how I was chosen for such an all-encompassing love, but I know that Jesus chose me, and I am forever grateful.

For me, as a woman in my fifties, married for thirty years, I have gradually come to understand that my vocation as a wife and mother is who I truly am, no matter how passionate I may be about the projects and people in the rest of my life. The married vocation is my path of sanctification and the perfect means for me to die to self and fall more deeply in love with God.

Married people walk a path of sanctification in their communion of persons. Through the sacrament of matrimony, they are called to love each other unconditionally and to help each other into heaven, bringing up children to know, love, and serve God. While the sacramental union of spouses can be extremely joyful, the married call is not about seeking personal happiness; it is about lovingly sacrificing for the happiness and well-being of the family and the community.

Ellen Gable Hrkach is a married mother of five, an author, and a longtime teacher of Natural Family Planning, along with her husband, James. Even after thirty-three years of marriage, Ellen has a great passion for her vocation as a wife and mother and believes that it is essential to keep the flames of love burning brightly. She describes a secret to marital success that flies in the face of popular culture's selfish ideals:

> "I am third," is a quote from Catherine Doherty, foundress of Madonna House, and it's a quote that I have displayed prominently above my desk: *God first, others second, myself third.* Self-sacrificial love, or putting our spouse's needs before our own needs, is an ideal way to keep the flame burning in a sacramental marriage. It's a choice to love the other, regardless of circumstances. When a couple is in a long-term, sacrificial, marital union, it's natural that the flame will keep burning because we want what is best for each other in all aspects of marital life.

Like the crucified Christ, our sacrificial love becomes a sign of God's love, made present in the world. Many women have had the experience of nursing a husband in his final days of life, sometimes through mental and physical incapacitation. It's a special kind of suffering when your spouse can no longer respond to your acts of kindness or doesn't recognize who you are.

There is no more powerful witness than the dedicated service of such women (and men), persevering in heroic patience and devotion through the aching loneliness of the final days, months, and years of a spouse's life. Surely Our Lord smiles down from the cross at such hidden heroism, tucked away in the monotony and stress of daily care-taking. Women in this situation need our love, prayers, and practical support, as they live out their vocation in this intensely challenging period of their lives.

Maturing Vocations

Mature vocations can be intense—in a good way. Susan Tassone is a single woman and the author of many books about devotion to the Holy Souls in purgatory. She has lived most of her adult life in service of the Church and finds her sixth decade to be one of deep passion and commitment, as well as a time of heightened appreciation for beauty and love. "You want to squeeze life tighter," she says with enthusiasm. When she visits her extended family and greets their young children, Susan scoops them up and twirls them around. "I'm noticing the intensity of my love for them. I squeeze my little cupcakes! Who they are is so precious," she says brightly. "They love the love!"

She points out the value of having older family members to dote on little ones, since busy young parents can sometimes forget, in the midst of so many distractions, to treasure each moment with their children. The ordinary solitude of her life as a writer sensitizes her to family dynamics, so she notices all the subtle ways that people overlook each other's needs for affection and attention. She tries to help them see each other more clearly, with gentle words of advice. "We're made for love and intimacy," she says. "Everybody wants love."

This increasing clarity and intensity seems to cross all boundaries of vocation and culture. Since professing her first vows more than forty years ago, Sister Bernarda says that her vocation has changed, too.

"It has grown deeper and more joyful as I have gotten to know him. Growing closer to God makes you happy!"

With maturity comes understanding and self-knowledge, too. Louise has come to see that her vocation fits her needs and personality:

> I'm a very social person, but I also have an affinity for solitude. I crave times of quiet prayer, and this vocation allows me the time to do that. I know God invited me to this vocation, and it suits me deeply because in his mysterious way I was created for this. I see great beauty in other ways of life, but this is the way of life he invited me to. It's not that I'm never frustrated or dry or questioning in how I live my call, but it satisfies that deepest part of me, so there is nothing else I'd rather be doing.

Maturity brings wisdom and confidence. Tracey advises sharing our knowledge with younger couples:

> We should pass on whatever good we have learned. Not a shortcut, not "tips." I don't want to say, "I'm older now, and I can show you how to do it the *easy* way." You don't want the easy way. Run the other way if someone says, "I know the easy way"! You get to a certain stage and you think you have it down pat: This is what we need to be happy. And then you get to your fifties, and you have that revelation of what's really important, and you get back to basics. You feel bad for people who don't have Christ in their lives. It's not a midlife crisis— it's a Christ crisis!

The Impact of Health on Vocation

Lisa Hendey, bestselling author and breast cancer survivor, is clear that even under ordinary circumstances, her physical well-being impacts the living out of her married vocation. She shares:

When we don't care for ourselves physically, we're weakened emotionally and psychologically in ways that impair our ability to perform our vocations effectively. If I've overeaten or over-consumed alcohol, it takes a toll on the work I can do to serve my husband and kids; it has an influence on my soul. You get yourself into a cycle of sin that just weighs you down.

Louise notes that, for the consecrated virgin living alone, illness or impairment is a frightening prospect that requires advanced planning, the support of family and friends, and most of all, great faith. She says, "I know I have to first and foremost rely on the Lord, but I also have to be proactive in finding people who are willing to be available when I need them." She has learned a lot from personal experience:

I recently went through a very frightening situation with vision problems. The doctors had tried lots of things but I was slowly—and then not so slowly—losing my vision. I spent a lot of wasted time envisioning myself stuck in my house, unable to drive and watching a lot of television because I was afraid I wouldn't be able to read.

Her time of suffering brought her closer to the Lord.

I needed to actively remember that my life belonged to God, and I begged him not only for the grace of physical sight but also for spiritual sight, so that no matter what happened I would trust in him and rely on his care. I'm happy to say that the one last surgery they could try worked fantastically, and my vision is much improved. I am grateful every day for this.

For the religious sister living in community, life is more serene. Asked about how her health affects her vocation, Sister Bernarda laughs and says that she will have "no retirement!" But illness, she says, teaches humility. "You see that if you died, someone would continue your work. You are not so important," she says, laughing. "When someone is sick, another will work harder in order to cover her, but it is not a problem. The one who works is not unhappy."

Setbacks and Temptations

In the early part of her religious life, Sister Bernarda experienced a time of profound suffering that she calls "a purification." She started to question her vocation. "I was so afraid of God. I thought, *How can I be a nun when I have so many weaknesses?* I didn't think he would ever bother with me. I didn't think that living a life totally for God was my place."

Whenever she saw a woman with a child during that period, it caused acute suffering. She worried that she had made a terrible mistake. As she continued to develop a relationship with God, she realized that her vocation was to be "a spiritual mother," and the dark period began to wane. It helped that a priest explained the soul's relationship to God as one of the beloved and "the Lover," recalling the spiritual poems of St. John of the Cross.[49] Sister Bernarda began to see God as love, rather than as a judge, and at last she found peace.

"I felt a void later and realized, *I need a mother.* So I knelt down in my little cell," she recalls with a chuckle, "and asked Mary to be my mother. My physical mother was home in Poland praying for me, but Mary became my mother, too. She brought me to Jesus, introduced me to his heart, his love."

Sister Bernarda leans closer, her eyes bright. "She is 'the woman,' not just a white plaster statue! She was tough. She pushed Jesus to begin his public life, pushed him toward the hour of the cross. What a faith! She said, 'Do whatever he tells you,' and these are her last words in the Bible."

Tracey, a natural mother and teacher, is a person of great depth. She lives out her vocation fully aware that the world is pounding out a marriage-destroying drumbeat for selfishness twenty-four hours a day, seven days a week. When I asked her about temptations and setbacks in the married vocation, she laughed and said, "I know this is going to sound corny, but marriage is like a horse show."

She described the way the horse and rider move around the obstacle course, first jumping the smaller hurdles and then working their way up to the more challenging ones. At some point, the horse's hoof might tip the hurdle, slightly, or the horse might even take a fall, and it will have to go around and try again. Tracey says that obstacles and temptations in marriage are like that. We go around the course with our spouse and take each hurdle, together. But when we mess up, we have to come around and keep trying until we get it right. Tracey equates this with the spiritual life, as well:

> Sometimes things happen and we don't have time to meditate on God before we make a decision. If I'm caught off-guard and the situation didn't go well, I meditate on it and ask God, "What should I have done?" Now, the world tells you, "Just brush it off. Move on. It'll take care of itself." The world isn't saying, "Wait a second. History is bound to repeat itself, so let's think about this. What would God want you to do? What can you do to rectify this for next time?"

Regarding married romance, Tracey says:

> The world has lied to all these couples—through TV shows, movies, books, and magazines—that everything's supposed to be wonderful and exciting all the time, and it's not true. Not that marriage isn't exciting and fun, but everything around

us says you don't have to suffer. That's all a lie. You're in this together. You're his sacrament and he's your sacrament.

Lisa Hendey adds:

Being with someone in difficult times, in illness or financial struggles, you are able to rise to the occasion in ways you might not think you could. Because of the way my husband loves me and I love him, it's easier to understand the concept of unconditional love. If human love can be this beautiful, how much more rich and full and beautiful is God's love than the love we experience in this life!

Louise is eloquent on the topic of overcoming setbacks in her vocation:

I think it is the same for someone living a consecrated single life as it is for anyone who is trying to live as a disciple of Christ. The primary way of overcoming difficulties is to cling more closely to Christ. As a consecrated person, I don't have a spouse or children to help me, so I have to dig more deeply into my relationship with the Lord, even when it feels like he is the one allowing me to struggle.

Faith and trust become big factors. It helps to make positive and active choices to do something that will set me in a more positive, faith-filled position. If I am lonely, I can take the initiative to contact someone. If I am angry, I can take the initiative to pray for whomever has angered me, rather than indulging in my anger. So, it is similar to anybody fighting a temptation—lots of truth applied to the situation and lots of humble surrender to God's grace.

Something I always laugh about is that if I am having a disagreement with my spouse, it has to be me that's the problem, since God is perfect. Sometimes it makes me dig my heels into my rebelliousness, but most often it makes me quicker to surrender my will because I know that sooner or later it will come down to that. And God is always so gracious with me in my struggles. He calls me to a deeper response, but he is very gentle and understanding of my weakness. His grace is everything.

When Disaster Strikes

When they were still young and lovely, both my grandmother and a beloved aunt were abandoned by their husbands, and they had to continue on alone, raising their children in poverty. Both remained chaste and faithful to their wedding vows in the face of the unthinkable: They and their children had been rejected by the men who had vowed to love and protect them.

My father remembers lying awake, as a young boy, listening to his full-time working mother ironing their school clothes before retiring for the night. She was poor, but she was proud, and she was determined that her children would go to school looking as clean and well cared for as any others. As she labored, exhausted and heartbroken, the ironing board creaked and mingled with the muffled sounds of her weeping.

The question must be asked: What do we do when our vocation seems to end due to circumstances beyond our control? A true vocation, of course, never really ends, but it may take a new form, and the transition may be painful and confusing. I think of the elderly nuns that my priest friend visits in a nursing home here in New York.

Some of them are wheelchair-bound and frail, no longer able to live out their religious vocations through service, as they did for so many years. But their vocations are honored in their willingness to persevere in faith to the end, offering their prayers and pains to God in the monotonous routines of each day. To the noisy, self-important world, these delicate creatures are invisible, their contributions seemingly nonexistent, but some day in heaven we will see the glories and miracles brought into being through their patient courage and selfless trust in Jesus.

The widow or the abandoned wife is similar. While she can no longer physically serve her absent spouse, she can, with God's help, honor her marital vows in her interior life. She can pray and offer her sufferings for her husband and children, and she can seek the sanctuary of her own heart, where God waits to comfort her. As she practices the intention of trust in God's divine plan for her life, he will strengthen her in the abundance of his grace.

God engages each of us, in every phase of our lives, in a conversation overflowing with his love. We might think of him communicating with us throughout our days, much the way we coo to our infants and tell stories to our children. They may not understand every word, but our care for them comes through and bathes their souls in love. God's tender attention to us is spoken through our experiences, our relationships, and our efforts to listen to him. Sometimes his word to us emerges out of suffering, lifting us up at turning points where we are weakened by discouragement and even tempted to despair. When we offer it all to him, trusting him to bring good out of every moment of our lives, he responds, blessing our vocations with overwhelming generosity and kindness.

Chapter Seven

DON'T TEMPT ME!
Three Common Pitfalls to Avoid

Do all things without grumbling or questioning.

—Philippians 2:14

Humble perseverance brings spiritual maturity, as we conquer the ordinary temptations of each day. Those victories bring us strength, wisdom, faith, and a radiant spirit of gratitude that keeps our lives exciting and our relationships healthy. I should point out that it is not a sin to be tempted along the way; it's part of the human condition that reaches all the way back to our first parents. Sometimes we experience an attraction to the dark comforts of sin, and the incomparable gift of our free will is tested. Let's look at a few of the most common temptations for women and some practical ways to avoid giving in to them.

Complain, Complain, Complain

I have a problem with complaining: I despise listening to it, and I hate catching myself doing it. I don't know about you, but especially if I'm overtired or stressed, I'm vulnerable to negative thinking. At the first sign of disappointment, frustration, or unexpected changes of plan, out pop the whiny comments and criticisms, falling like acid rain on the people around me. When I'm feeling this way, I'm sorely tempted to the sins of gossip and ingratitude, as well, and I risk drawing others into sin, right along with me.

Let's look to the Bible for some pointers on why this is an important topic. First, complaining runs counter to the fruits of the Holy Spirit and a healthy Christian mindset. We are called to "live by the Spirit" and to focus our thoughts on everything good, beautiful, and "worthy of praise" (see Philippians 4:8).

We were not made adopted sisters of our crucified Lord just to waste our precious lives cataloguing and protesting our own crosses. In Galatians St. Paul tells us that human beings fall easily into "enmity, strife, jealousy, anger, selfishness, dissensions, party spirit..." but "the fruit of the Spirit is love, joy, peace, patience, kindness, goodness, faithfulness, gentleness, self-control" (Galatians 5:20, 22–23). We need divine help to overcome temptation, but there are steps we can take toward freedom from the habit of complaint.

Allow me to offer a gigantic understatement: I have not yet reached perfection in this area, but I've noticed that it's very hard to complain about something that has been offered to God for some greater purpose. For instance, if you are married and it makes you jumpy when your otherwise gentle and kind husband cracks his knuckles or yells at the TV, try offering your acceptance of his irksome habits for a lonesome widow or a woman wounded by divorce who has more than her share of peace and quiet. There's always someone in need of your sacrifice, and the cross of Christ has eloquently demonstrated the power of pain suffered out of love to bring about positive change. We become members of his body through our baptism, so our small offerings actually help save the world, a little at a time.

If you exchange your right to complain for an attitude of sacrifice, you'll find that what was formerly an irritating situation suddenly becomes sanctified and meaningful, and you'll be freer to express your appreciation and affection to the good man waiting for you on the couch, the querulous elderly relative, or the demanding supervisor. Where a spirit of loving sacrifice and self-mastery reigns, love blossoms and transforms us, making us channels of healing and conversion.

God rushes into the empty space where our self-interest was previously enthroned, filling our lives with mystery and meaning.

As often as possible, it's helpful to take our frustrations and hurts and spiritually lay them on the altar at Mass, or simply offer them to God within our own hearts. For instance, we might give Jesus the aches and pains of our bodies as penance for our sins, or cheerfully perform a tedious task while we ask him to reduce the suffering of a soul in purgatory. Of course, we should also ask him for the grace to accept our suffering patiently and willingly. By acting generously in moments of affliction, we ennoble our souls while we benefit others in surprising ways. I'll give you a personal example.

One day long ago, I was at my wit's end with someone close to me. Full of bitterness, heartbroken, and complaining to God in tears, suddenly the unthinkable occurred to me: I would lovingly offer the pain of that deep wound for the good of the person who had made me so unhappy, with no strings or conditions attached. I would simply accept the pain as a sacrifice of love. Don't be too impressed; I couldn't believe I was even considering such a thing! To do so went against my every human instinct, and yet the thought was so compelling that I knew it was right, and I recognized it as an invitation from God.

As soon as I made the offering, a strange quiet came over me. I no longer felt helpless and victimized. I felt the power of God's love surge through me, and courage filled my heart. If you're wondering what happened to the source of my pain—well, it took time, but the relationship in question experienced many beautiful, incremental healings in the days and years to come. I sincerely believe that God rewarded my offering, that when I asked him to bless my loved one with a degree of mercy that seemed outlandish and unfair, he enriched my life beyond my wildest expectations.

It was a turning point in my life, a gift given to me at a time when I had no wisdom and little virtue of my own. Because, in that moment of grace, I was willing to act against my natural instincts of self-interest and my worldly principles of fairness and justice, God gifted me with the strength to perform a small, hidden act of heroic love—for the first time in my life. That brief moment was a game changer. It was the beginning of the realization that suffering truly has redemptive power, and that the cross of Jesus Christ can and should be the center of my life. It showed me that merely being open to the guidance of the Holy Spirit could flood my life with transforming miracles.

That small moment broke through the entrenched belief that I should always be able to reason my way through life's tough questions and provided a glimpse into the mysterious wisdom of our loving God. This one lesson did much to strengthen my newfound faith in a supernatural Father who knew my soul better than I knew myself and who knew how to break down my resistance with the gentlest of nudges. It gave me a taste for mystery and an increased willingness to step into the unknown, as long as it was in partnership with God. Life became an adventure to me, as my eyes were opened to my own littleness enfolded tenderly in God's infinite love.

Decades later, in his 2013 encyclical letter, *Lumen Fidei* (The Light of Faith), our Holy Father, Pope Francis, wrote this:

> A light this powerful cannot come from ourselves but from a more primordial source: in a word, it must come from God. Faith is born of an encounter with the living God who calls us and reveals his love, a love which precedes us and upon which we can lean for security and for building our lives. Transformed by this love, we gain fresh vision, new eyes to see; we realize that it contains a great promise of fulfillment, and that a vision

of the future opens up before us. Faith, received from God as a supernatural gift, becomes a light for our way, guiding our journey through time.[50]

The Holy Father's words confirmed for me that we are truly blind until God gives us sight, but that when we open to his healing light, he pours it on, empowering and transforming our lives for the better.

On the Bright Side

Since God waits eagerly to grant us this light of faith, and since his arms are loaded up with gifts of grace to strengthen that faith and bring it to fruition, it makes sense for us to make every effort to live our lives in and through that wondrous radiance. But to live in the bright precincts of a living faith means cultivating what motivational expert Zig Ziglar called an "attitude of gratitude."[51]

Counting blessings does indeed sweep away discouragements, but it does so much more. Cultivating gratitude sensitizes our souls to beauty. It's like any virtue; the more we practice it, the more we benefit. Making a habit of appreciating the many blessings in our lives changes us profoundly, bringing the shining certainty of God's presence into every moment of our lives. The more we pay attention to his gifts, the more we are empowered to see of the love, light, beauty, goodness, and truth he supplies. The more we contemplate these priceless gifts, the more we become natural purveyors of joy and beauty to the world.

Almighty God looks back at us when we contemplate his generosity, opening a radiant gateway to conversing with him in tender intimacy. Especially when we are suffering, praising and thanking God for his goodness releases a deluge of graces into our lives. In his letter to the Thessalonians, St. Paul guides his flock with these beautiful words: "Rejoice always, pray constantly, give thanks in all circumstances; for this is the will of God in Christ Jesus for you. Do not quench the Spirit" (1 Thessalonians 5:16–19).

This same attitude of looking for what is good and beautiful around us is important for all of our human relationships, as well as our relationship with God. Over time, failings of personality or character in someone close to us can become vexing and may morph from annoying quirks into full-blown crosses. However, if we take a strong, positive stand from the start and make a sustained effort to see the beauty and goodness that is present in every child of God, we accomplish something powerful: We value the gift that our families, neighbors, and colleagues represent in our lives and avoid squandering the opportunity to bring them blessings.

In *Story of a Soul*, St. Thérèse shares an insight drawn from this line of Scripture: "Greater love has no man than this, that a man lay down his life for his friends" (John 15:13). She writes:

> When meditating on these words of Jesus, I understood how imperfect was my love for my Sisters in religion. I saw I didn't love them as God loves them. *Ah! I understand now that charity consists in bearing with the faults of others, in not being surprised at their weakness, in being edified by the smallest acts of virtue we see them practice.*[52]

If we make even a modicum of effort to overlook the foibles of others, to assume the best motives possible, and to allow even their smallest acts of virtue to lift our spirits, God blesses us abundantly. When we forget ourselves, he remembers us; when we die to selfishness, we live powerfully in grace.

If the chance to offer a foundation of tender acceptance to those you love has long since passed, seek sacramental reconciliation, and ask for God's help to reorient your attitude. He will reward your desire with the graces necessary to make lasting changes, heal you of chronic resentment, and bring peace. If someone you love has already passed on to God, have Masses offered for his or her soul. We can still love our dear departed ones and do them great good with our prayers and sacrifices. Ask God to help you forgive any wrong they have done to you or to others. Forgive them their debts, and God will forgive yours.

Obviously, if someone close to you has fallen into serious misconduct, immorality, addiction, or despair, it is important to seek wise counsel for ways of gently guiding them back to healing and hope. We're not meant to ignore each other's unspoken cries for help; but we have a greater chance of success when we commit to seeing the best in others, in spite of their failings. They'll sense our regard for all that is good in them, however small it may seem to us, and will be more likely to accept our loving efforts to help.

Compare Equals Despair

We tend to project a persona to the world that is not altogether real, for lots of reasons. I think most often we're either afraid of being judged or we're a little addicted to being admired. We try not to risk anyone discovering just how weird or inadequate we really are. The reverse is also a problem. Isn't it true that we assume that, unlike us, the people we meet on social media or watch on television have it all together? Don't their vacations and vocations look happier, their homes and offices more beautiful? Aren't their thoughts more sublime, their social and spiritual lives more rewarding? Do you ever wonder if God loves them more? It seems a bit silly, now that I've written it all down, but these are all traps I've fallen into at various times!

What Jesus asks of each of us is entirely between the individual soul and his heart. No one else's spiritual or emotional or intellectual progress has any bearing at all on where God is calling us in the present moment—none whatsoever. We need to discern where he is drawing us along the path to heaven and keep our eyes on him. Constantly looking around and comparing ourselves to others leads to a lot of self-inflicted misery. Can you imagine what a wasted opportunity it would be if an Olympic swimmer dove into her lane at the sound of the starting pistol but kept turning her head to see where her opponents were in the other lanes? She'd end up in last place, her own potential abandoned through the indulgence of constantly comparing her progress with others'.

The more ordinary result of all this comparing is that human beings fall into jealousy and resentment, largely over false impressions. I find this very amusing, but St. Thérèse observed that some people become twisted up in resentment when they meet a very holy person. "When they see a soul more enlightened than others, immediately they conclude that Jesus loves them less than this soul, and that they cannot be called to the same perfection."

Thérèse goes on to say, rather indignantly, "Since when has the Lord *no longer the right* to make use of one of His creatures to dispense necessary nourishment to souls whom He loves?"[53] In other words, he loves us so much that he sends saints into our lives to teach us, to feed us with love and wisdom, to draw us closer to his heart, which is starved for our love. When we assume God loves a holy person more than he loves us, we miss the point and lose the gift that was wrapped so beautifully on our behalf!

The truth is, if you scratch the surface of anyone's life, especially the ones you think are the most perfect, you will find suffering, insecurity, and sin. How often do picture-perfect celebrity marriages disintegrate? How often do the wealthy have to hire criminal defense lawyers? How many times have you gotten to know someone you believed to "have it all," only to discover she carries crosses so heavy that all your envy dried up in an instant?

We all experience the brokenness of our own humanity, and no one's life—this bears repeating—*no one's life* is perfect. To some degree, every single human being on the planet takes shelter behind a presentable mask to hide the uncomfortable truth that they are embarrassingly broken and in need of healing. Comparing ourselves to what we think we see in others is often no different than comparing ourselves to fictional characters in a novel.

It's very difficult, as human beings, to avoid the problem of comparisons, but the solution always comes back to accepting and offering our imperfect lives to God and thanking him for his many blessings. Counting blessings every day resurrects our joy and puts all our perceived inadequacies in perspective. False ideas of perfection are like the hamster wheel that exhausts us and takes us nowhere, but putting our attention as kindly as possible on the goodness and beauty of our own lives takes us off the wheel and onto the path of joy and peace.

Ponder this: God contains within himself the entire universe—the nebulas and stars, the planets and galaxies, the earth with its splendid multitude of natural wonders, all of the glories of heaven, every shining angel and holy saint, and every loved one who has gone to be with God. All that is winsome, holy, lovely, healing, illuminating, and true is contained in him. And he lives in all his infinite perfection and power in *your soul*. Think of the magnitude of that presence, carried within you. Allow it to fill you up with awe. Then praise God, perhaps praying with the psalmist: "You formed my inmost being; you knit me in my mother's womb. I praise you, because I am wonderfully made; wonderful are your works!" (Psalm 139:13–14).

Forgiveness as a Lifestyle

Before my conversion in 1992, I was a bitter person. I wallowed in resentment and lived almost continually in a state of suppressed rage.

Blame was my game, and "martyr" was my identity. It was horrible and eventually drove me to the brink of despair. I remember writing in my journal one day, attempting to describe my feelings. The image that came to me was of a powerful destructive force exploding outward from my body into the universe, disintegrating everything in its path. I had good reasons for feeling the way I did. I just didn't know that all that pent-up rage and chronic resentment were slowly destroying me.

There's a saying that is variously attributed to Emmet Fox, Nelson Mandela, Buddha, and others, which goes something like this: "Resentment is like drinking poison and then waiting for the other person to die." When we nurture unforgiveness in our hearts, we become toxic and self-destructive in our thinking. When we focus on another person's faults, we stop growing and moving forward, and *we miss the adventure of our own lives*. Conversely, when we endeavor to truly forgive, it's like learning to fly.

When I first came back to the Catholic faith, years ago, I was fascinated by the notion of forgiveness. Humanly speaking, there was no way I could set aside all the hurt and dysfunction of my life and simply move on, but because I was reading Catholic books and listening to great talks for the very first time, the concept of asking God for the graces necessary to help me forgive captured my imagination. I was praying the Our Father daily and saying the words, "Forgive us our trespasses *as* we forgive those who trespass against us," and it started to hit me that unhealed emotional wounds were standing in my way. I needed to change my lifestyle from one of enslavement to the past to one of freedom and forgiveness.

God was very generous. Even though my earliest pleas for help were made half-heartedly, he blessed me for asking and richly rewarded those awkward beginnings. I noticed, almost immediately, that even people who lived hundreds of miles away were opening up to me, being kinder, and—in ways that had nothing to do with me—growing and maturing, becoming people I actually found easier to love. It occurred to me that the instant I chose to try to forgive, it was like spiritual chains had been removed from those I was asking God to release from my debt. As it turns out, it wasn't just me being held back by my bitterness; in some strange way, I was discovering that we are all connected, and my unforgiveness was a stumbling block for them, too.

A dear friend once shared that whenever she feels hurt by someone else's behavior, she silently prays, "Jesus, please forgive me for the times I have done this to you." The practice began many years ago, when she handed her toddler a slice of peach and watched him drop it to the floor and stomp on it. She remembers, "I felt a surge of rage, and at that moment I had this visceral visual [image] of the rage God must feel, having given me two sweet little kids and watching me stomp on them emotionally every time I reacted angrily toward them." It was one of those moments of grace that became a gateway to spiritual maturity and led to greater peace in her life.

God gradually peeled away my own bitterness, layer by layer, and brought his healing, life-giving light to the dark, infected places in my heart. It was and is a slow, subtle process, but experiencing the refreshment of God's mercy unlocked my personal prison. In forgiveness, I was free at last.

Obsessing about Loss of Youth

Charm is deceitful, and beauty is vain;
  but a woman who fears the Lord is to be praised.
—Proverbs 31:30

I remember how contemptuous I was, as a young woman, looking at photos of celebrities and socialites whose addiction to plastic surgery had rendered them almost inhuman looking. With skin stretched so tight their faces were frozen in ghoulish smiles, they inspired my disgust, not my compassion. It wasn't until I hit midlife and the skin over my eyes and under my chin started to sag that I understood the pain and suffering behind the surgeries. Now, when I see those same pictures, I want to give someone a hug, not a lecture.

For women, aging can feel like a series of unpleasant surprises, but obsessing about the loss of our vitality and superficial beauty is a counterproductive waste of our time. The alternative, clinging to God's timeless and powerful presence within us, ensures that our true beauty continues to bear radiant and holy fruit throughout our lives.

When I was interviewing women for this book, Catholic author and biblical scholar Sarah Christmyer was kind enough to share an illuminating insight into beauty and aging:

> Real beauty is on the inside, and it really starts to show when our outer beauty fades. I saw that first hand when my mother's mother was dying of cancer and I lived with her for a couple of years. Sometimes I'd wake up hearing her during the night, and my first thought was that she was crying in pain; but she was pouring her heart out in prayer for other people. I started to see her body like a clay pot, full of God's love. The more "cracked" it got with illness, the more God's glory shone out from inside. Cancer and chemo aren't kind to the body; but she was the most beautiful woman I knew.

Sarah's image resonated with me. My mom, Barbara Kirkwood, was brought up in poverty by a single mother and was teased in school because she wore hand-me-down clothes from her Protestant church's charity bin. She went to Sunday services by herself for years, and she participated in plays and choirs, finding great comfort in her love of God and the community of the faithful. When she and my dad got engaged, she took instruction in the Catholic faith and fell in love all over again. Her Catholic faith has sustained her through a great many trials over the years, and she has developed the kind of mental toughness that totally precludes self-pity, no matter what problems she faces.

She's in her eighties now, but about fifteen years ago she was diagnosed with an aggressive form of breast cancer and had a mastectomy. I tease her that she was so matter-of-fact about it she behaved as though she were only having her shrubs pruned. I'm certain I would have been a total drama queen, if it had been my procedure. "I wanted to live," she says, simply, shrugging and smiling. "And Daddy was a big help." She moved on from traumatic surgery that, for many women, leaves them feeling less womanly and less "themselves." Not so for my courageous mom. She keeps her eye on what's really important and lets go of the rest, allowing the beauty of her interior life to shine through.

My mother-in-law, Margot, is in her nineties and is still bright-eyed and full of enthusiasm for life; however, she is coming to terms with a noticeable loss of physical energy and stamina, due to congestive heart failure.

As we chatted about accepting the changes in our bodies as we age, she sighed only briefly, knowing that to dwell on loss is counterproductive. Raised during the Great Depression, a World War II veteran, and a cancer survivor twice over, Margot doesn't waste her life bemoaning old age, widowhood, or any other of life's tough breaks. She simply adjusts her expectations and moves on to the next opportunity with enthusiasm.

Such women are heroines to me, and I want to be just like them when I grow up. Growing old with those we love becomes a great privilege when we have spent a lifetime learning to appreciate the value of those who have walked with us along life's journey. If our lives have been lived with love—however imperfectly—aging is not a shock or a terrible burden to us, but a natural season to be treasured along with our beautiful memories.

Of course, we may well resent the stiffness in our joints, the aches and pains, and the sad passing of loved ones, but if we take care along the way to treasure our blessings, appreciate our friends, and give ourselves generously to others, old age can be a time of joy and peace. With the knowledge that we have honored God in our relationships and endeavored to be a gift to others, a certain quiet satisfaction tempers our sorrows and brings us a holy strength. And that's beautiful.

Chapter Eight

CULTURE SHOCK

Some Roadblocks to Peace and How to Avoid Them

Peace I leave with you; my peace I give to you; not as the world gives do I give to you. Let not your hearts be troubled, neither let them be afraid.

—John 14:27

I love my computer and my smartphone, but it's important to shut them off and take time for people and prayer. Most days, I spend hours writing, managing my web presence, doing research, or teaching my online courses. I enjoy texting friends and loved ones, keeping up with news and commentary, and checking in with the myriad fascinating conversations taking place via social media. In fact, I start each day in prayer using devotions saved to my desktop. I found most of them online. It's easier to stay organized that way, and it helps me to establish a God-centered rhythm to my day. But some days, I look more at a screen than I do at the world around me.

Overuse of "screen time" can cause real damage to our brains, our emotional lives, and our relationships. Studies have shown that too much time attending to a computer screen or smartphone can create an addictive urge to constantly check and recheck for updates,[54] whether via e-mail or other forms of social media. In the process, important tasks and relationships are neglected. Regular computer use has been shown to reduce our attention spans,[55] disrupt our sleep,[56] and cause or exacerbate problems with anxiety and depression.[57] Computers are amazing, wonderful tools. However, we need to be careful not to stay too long in the virtual world, since Our Lord is gently whispering in our hearts to come away to a quiet place.

Pope Emeritus Benedict XVI, in his 2009 message for World Communications Day, cautioned against some of these dangers:

> It would be sad if our desire to sustain and develop *on-line* friendships were to be at the cost of our availability to engage with our families, our neighbours and those we meet in the daily reality of our places of work, education and recreation. If the desire for virtual connectedness becomes obsessive, it may in fact function to isolate individuals from real social interaction while also disrupting the patterns of rest, silence and reflection that are necessary for healthy human development.[58]

Pace Yourself

Our lives are increasingly complicated and distracting, as women in the second half of life carry heavy loads in their families and communities. The pace of living seems to get faster every year, just as we may be craving some down time. Because our hearts are generous and receptive to the needs of others, we tend to be caretakers, advocates, and surrogate mothers, in and out of our families, in the home and in the workplace. The day-to-day demands can be stressful.

According to a recent study by the Pew Research Center[59] middle-aged adults are increasingly "sandwiched" between their teenaged or young adult children and their parents, often providing housing and financial support to both generations simultaneously. Add together the cost of their children's education, care of grandchildren and grandparents, and their own rising medical costs, and the second half of life becomes a time of heavy challenge.

Even if everything is going well, it's usually because we're working very hard to keep all the various parts of our lives running smoothly. I think of a circus performer spinning a dozen plates, simultaneously, without any falling. When it's all going as planned, it gives the illusion of being easy, but keeping it all in balance requires total commitment and concentration.

With women, I know we often feel that if we stop attending to any of the many balancing acts we continually negotiate, a "plate" will drop, and our lives will be in disarray. I often find myself catching a falling plate just before it hits the floor. I might be making a writing deadline in the midst of a family crisis or overnighting a bill about to come due. When a near miss occurs, I wonder, *Is my self-image too caught up in this constant motion, or is this simply the challenge of living life to the full?*

However happy our lives may be, our spiritual lives can be seriously challenged by the constant demands on our time and mental capacities. When we're tired and stretched thin, falling out of the habit of prayer can lead to burnout and feelings of being overwhelmed by life. It may seem a strange observation, but we can get a little *prideful* about keeping it all going.

We can get into the habit of relying on ourselves too heavily, mostly because we're moving too fast to ask for help. We know we need to stop to pray. But to put on the brakes, to stop and empty ourselves before God and beg for grace, takes humility and resolve. On some level, we think the world relies on our strength, but our true strength is found in prayer.

God often speaks to us in a gentle voice that is easily overlooked and ignored in our noisy, dramatic world. The Bible tells us that, in a time of great danger and distress, the prophet Elijah was hiding in a cave on Mount Horeb, where he was told to wait for a visitation from God. One after another, God sent impressive commotions to rattle his frightened prophet: first, a destructive hurricane that shattered the mountainside, next an earthquake, and then a raging fire. Elijah, however, sensed that God's voice was not speaking through the tumult, so he continued to wait. Finally, he was rewarded with a gentle breeze, which caused him to cover his head in reverence, as it drew him out of the cave and into the presence of God (see 1 Kings 19:11–13).

Like Elijah, we need to discern what God's voice may be whispering to our souls. Even in the most hectic life, we can open our hearts to small moments of contact with God by keeping our prayer lives simple. In fact, prayer can be so basic that it can occur in the midst of our activities, in the privacy of our hearts.

Fr. Robert Spitzer, S.J., wrote a wonderful book for busy people,[60] in which he explored the use of brief, spontaneous aspirations as a powerful form of prayer. When calling out to God in the midst of crisis or worry, he tells us, it is efficacious to express no more than the words "Help" or "Have mercy." Other suggestions include praying the Hail Mary and announcing, "I give up, Lord. You take care of it." (That one made me laugh.)

St. Thérèse of Lisieux had trouble with long, formal prayers. Some of them actually gave her a headache! She described her own childlike prayers as a "glance" heavenward:

> I say very simply to God what I wish to say, without composing beautiful sentences, and He always understands me. For me, *prayer* is an aspiration of the heart, it is a simple glance directed to heaven, it is a cry of gratitude and love in the midst of trial as well as joy; finally, it is something great, supernatural, which expands my soul and unites me to Jesus.[61]

As much as I crave her simplicity, I recognize that Thérèse's life of devotion grew out of the habit of structured prayer within her religious community. After the morning offering, my favorite practice is the daily recitation of the rosary, which I can accomplish while driving and listening to a rosary CD on busy days. Even a few minutes of mental prayer, praising and thanking God, can be a sweet and encouraging time of refreshment. A little regular Scripture reading can bring a powerful awareness of God's presence throughout the day.

Pope Benedict devoted many of his homilies to the practice of *Lectio Divina*, which he described this way: "It consists in pouring over a biblical text for some time, reading it and rereading it, as it were, 'ruminating' on it as the Fathers say and squeezing from it, so to speak, all its 'juice,' so that it may nourish meditation and contemplation and, like water, succeed in *irrigating life itself.*" [62]

As busy as the Holy Father's active pontificate must have been, he made time to soak in the soul-irrigating waters of contemplation. We can do the same. God's holy Word is a living expression of his love for us, so any time at all spent opening our hearts to his promptings in Scripture is beneficial to our souls. By reverently inviting the assistance of the Holy Spirit, we receive clarity and wisdom that illuminate our complicated lives. To draw boundary lines that protect and nurture our prayer time is an act of self-preservation, especially in a media-driven culture that chips away at our dignity as daughters of God.

Impurity Is All Around Us

To be a savvy consumer of culture, it's important to stay aware of the messaging of contemporary media, because it can affect us more than we realize. Movies, television, and advertising too often embrace behaviors and fashions that objectify and degrade our feminine dignity. The language of love is often made synonymous with promiscuity and broken vows, as fictional characters move from one affair to another without suffering realistic consequences. Faithful vocations to marriage or religious life are spuriously framed as prisons for the human spirit, when, in reality, selfless devotion is the neglected, narrow path to the most fulfilling mysteries of our lives. Life, as seen through the camera's lens, can very attractively promote an upside-down version of reality. What is sinful and destructive for the human heart is presented as beautiful, and what is lovely and holy is mocked.

To allow the culture to mislead us about our identity as daughters of God has an impact on more than just us. We are the hearts of our homes and communities, creators and caretakers of tradition, and mentors of generations to come. As women go, so goes any culture. Venerable Archbishop Fulton J. Sheen stated, "Since a woman is loved, it follows that the nobler a woman is, the nobler man will have to be to be deserving of that love. That is why the level of any civilization is always the level of its womanhood."[63]

The first time I read that quote, I had to read it over several times and reflect on my own beliefs. When I was in college in the late 1970s, I was taught that women were principally victims of an abusive male system that feared their strength and sought to dominate them. As I matured, I found that, indeed, some men and certain cultural tendencies were misguided, but that many men were fine and complicated individuals. It became apparent that to lump them all together was unfair and very often untrue.

Being aware of problems in society can never justify scapegoating any category of persons. We make our best impact when we use our feminine gifts to treat others as individuals whom God has placed in our paths, both to teach us and to learn from our example. Likewise, if we make the mistake of seeing ourselves as victims, we become vulnerable to manipulation by those who lead us away from our true strengths in order to control us. Too often, those who claim to represent women encourage them to seek a false "equality" by adopting the worst of male behaviors: promiscuity, aggression, unbridled ambition, and self-destructive addictions. Women have the power to guide the culture to a better place through their own standards of behavior and by setting expectations for others.

I remember driving by a local school when my daughter was about five years old. Spray-painted on a traffic sign in front of the building was the "F" word. A new reader, she asked me what it meant. A quick prayer preceded the answer that satisfied her: "It's an ugly word for something beautiful."

The "F" word perverts meaning, making a holy gift from God—our sexuality—into a dirty joke. Now I'd like to reverse that notion, for the sake of taking the idea of "perverted meaning" a little further. Many in the media have perverted the word *beauty*—which in its essence belongs to God—in order to cause something ugly: your own self-hatred. This word *beauty*, which ought to immediately direct our hearts to heaven itself, is distorted and repackaged for the sake of promoting a profitable lie. Hollywood's narcissistic and promiscuous ideals have upended concepts of true love and added to the confusion of a lonely and misguided populace. Movies and films threaten to alienate us from the holy language of real beauty and replace it with a kind of psychological and emotional cuss word.

For instance, if I am convinced by the behavior of fictional characters that promiscuity is a sign of personal freedom, I become very easy to control, abuse, and discard. And if beauty is sold as a commodity, rather than a God-given gift to every woman, I become an enslaved consumer, unable to take joy in the true beauty of authentic femininity.

Our beauty and sexuality are closely bound up in our identity as women, so the materialistic ethos behind popular culture hits us where we live, and it hits us hard. We need to get in the driver's seat and stay there.

This is not just a problem of maturing women. Our culture is obsessed with an artificial sense of beauty that has led many a young and lovely girl to starve herself to death, or to binge and purge in a compulsive ritual of self-hatred. I have known and loved some of these young women, and they were quite beautiful enough to start with; however, indoctrinated by false ideas of physical perfection, they just couldn't see their own beauty for themselves.

Sadly, many women have been tricked into exploiting themselves and their daughters for the sake of modernity and popularity, through immodest dress and behavior. They believe their bodies should be increasingly on display and that their sexuality is something to be "expressed" freely; that inspiring lust in men makes them healthy and powerful.

The false freedoms promised by Hollywood and the world of sexual politics are leading girls and women into sexual slavery through the normalized expectation of promiscuity and the lack of respect and commitment this practice encourages in men. Tragically, men, in turn, have become just as confused and hurt. Many have lost touch with their innate, God-given strength and the desire to protect and provide for women and children. Instead, they have fallen into a consumerist attitude. The children who result from these bankrupt unions are victimized in countless ways, including abandonment and abortion.

When everyone is objectified, everyone is victimized. Reverence for the sacredness of who we are, a true union of body and soul made in the image of a totally self-donating God, is destroyed through impurity. We can see how the chain reaction disrupts healthy relationships.

Without the stabilizing influences of grace and wisdom, women become part of a wider societal problem. "When mama ain't happy, ain't nobody happy," as the saying goes. And when "mama" isn't sure of her own identity and value in the eyes of God, nobody is sure of who they are anymore.

Our feminine beauty is so often misused because of its intense attractiveness and vulnerability. Watch the Super Bowl sometime, and count the number of commercials that feature pretty girls dressed to inspire lust, behaving seductively—never mind the cheerleaders at such games. If your friends, husband, or brothers are prone to gazing unreflectively at such images, remind them that each one of these young women is somebody's "little girl." Try, without rancor, to give them a fresh perspective.

Along with the prophets and saints of our spiritual history, we should feel very free to embrace our own desire to stand apart and rebel against the status quo. Regardless of the worrisome influences gaining traction in our society, our bodies remain worthy of reverence and respect. While there are undoubtedly some conscientious men who avert their eyes at such exploitation, too many viewers are encouraged to think of women as commodities to be consumed vicariously. We, however, can use our influence to lovingly impact the way our families think about and consume media.

You will meet with resistance, but it's important to speak up. Consider the impact of pornography around the globe, and try to imagine what our world would be like if only human beings understood our own longings. We are witnessing an epidemic of indescribably tragic proportions, a costly obsession with degraded sexuality that social scientists tell us will only get worse with the passage of time.

Placed on par with heroin addiction,[64] scientists warn that "erototoxins" released in the brain while viewing erotic materials affect mental function in much the same way as a narcotic high. This effect makes the urge irresistible and increasingly difficult to satisfy. The emotional and behavioral damages to men, women, and children are incalculable, as many who unknowingly long for God are sidetracked into darkness. This is an area that needs our constant prayers and sacrifices. We are a human family, and what hurts any part of society hurts us all.

Entering into the Presence of Purity

In a brief account in the Gospel of St. Matthew (see Matthew 9:20–22), a woman who has suffered from a hemorrhage for twelve years stealthily approaches Jesus in a crowd and touches the hem of his garment. She is instantly healed, even though to touch the rabbi was forbidden to women, especially when experiencing a flow of blood. In those days, and even in Orthodox Judaism today, a woman who is bleeding is considered a spiritual danger to men, since blood is so closely linked with death. After her menses cease, only the holy waters of the *mikvah*, or ritual bath, can allow her contact with her own husband.

In the Gospel account, a woman who likely believes herself to be in a similarly "impure" state approaches the most pure Jesus, seeking healing. She comes up behind him, because she is desperate and afraid of being rejected. Yet, in her great faith, she hopes that just touching the hem of his garment will bring forth an outpouring of divine power and she will finally be made whole.

We can assume that when Jesus turned to her and spoke, she must have been startled and even frightened. She may have expected that this sudden confrontation would end in a harsh and humiliating rebuke. In his tenderness and complete understanding, however, he merely said, "Courage, daughter! Your faith has saved you." In this stunning moment, a suffering woman encountered God's love for her, and Purity Himself became the cure for her desperation, sickness, and impurity.

There is nothing that cannot be swallowed up by God's love and cleansed, bringing us new life and new hope. God is our source, our life, our love, and our ultimate goal. Impurity is all around us, distracting us from what is of God and debasing that which is beautiful and radiant in our feminine humanity. Without an awareness of God, we simply cannot know ourselves.

Contrary to the popular lie that indulging in impure behavior, media, or thinking is nothing more than harmless recreation, impurity is incredibly destructive. Author John O'Donohue writes, "There is an unseemly coarseness to our times which robs the grace from our textures of language, feeling and presence."[65] Objectifying other human beings for our own amusement makes us self-centered and diminishes our ability to feel compassion and empathy for others. Purity, on the other hand, is a gateway into the presence of God, who is the very perfection of holy purity and compassion. The more we grow in purity, the closer we draw to Divine Love; therefore, where our own purity increases, so does our capacity to love.

Still, we are going to be tempted to impurity, even after going to confession and asking God for help. That's why it's important to practice what the Church calls "custody of the eyes": to avert our eyes when the behavior or dress of others tempts us to linger too long and dwell in sinful thoughts. I know that every time my daughter and I simply walk through our local mall, we find ourselves turning our heads away from gigantic photographs in shop windows, featuring nearly-nude young men and women who are, ironically, selling clothing. If I'm watching a movie and a sexually explicit scene begins, I close my eyes and pray until it is over.

The *Catechism of the Catholic Church* contains a beautiful section that unpacks the ninth commandment, which forbids covetous or lustful behavior (see 2514–2533). Just to skim through the summary at the end of the chapter reminds us that it is through purity that we are enabled to "see God" and to "see things according to God" (*CCC* 2531). "Purification of the heart demands prayer, the practice of chastity, purity of intention, and of vision. Purity of heart requires the modesty which is patience, decency, and discretion. Modesty protects the intimate center of the person" (*CCC* 2532–2533). The Catholic ideal of wholesome sexuality recognizes the dignity of the whole person and demands our respect and love.

My husband and I lived in Hong Kong during the mid-1990s, and we took the opportunity to do some traveling. While we were in Nepal for a few weeks, we became accustomed to placing our hands together, close to our hearts, fingertips pointing up, and bowing our heads slightly, whenever we greeted another person. "*Namaste*" (nah-mah-stay) is the most common greeting and roughly means, "I salute the divine in you." I'm not recommending that we adopt this practice, but truly, if we believe that God abides in us, we should be reverencing his presence in every person we meet.

As creators and guardians of culture, women are in the perfect position to help turn the cultural tide away from obscenity and back to the holy purity in which our minds, hearts, and souls thrive. If we set the standards high and encourage other women to do the same, our society will experience a seismic shift. We can choose to do battle by joining organizations that fight for wholesome values within our parishes and communities, and we should ask for the grace to persevere in the virtue of purity in our private lives.

And don't despair at your own imperfect purity. If your way of comporting yourself in dress, body language, speech, or even in your thoughts, feels like it needs a little fine-tuning, throw yourself into the arms of the Blessed Mother, the Virgin Most Pure, and ask for some guidance. Little by little, with great affection for you as her spiritual daughter, she will bring healing and insight and help you to unearth the beauty and purity of your God-given femininity. Her aim is always to bring us closer to Jesus, the source of all that is pure and radiant. She is never too busy to listen to your concerns or place her arm comfortingly around your shoulder. She loves you, and she delights in helping you to be your most holy, happy self.

Praying the rosary, which draws our hearts into meditations on certain key Gospel mysteries and deepens our relationship with Mary as our Mother, has been one of the most powerful influences in my life. I turn to Our Lady whenever impure thoughts or impulses assail me. Since, before my conversion, I occasionally watched or read impure materials, my imagination was scarred, making my mind a place of struggle against sinful thoughts. Calling out to Mary in the silence of my heart is a great help, and meditating on the mysteries of the rosary has been transformative.

Sister Lucia, one of the visionaries of Fatima, revealed this lesson from the apparition of Our Lady:

> The Most Holy Virgin in these last times in which we live has given a new efficacy to the recitation of the Holy Rosary. She has given this efficacy to such an extent that there is no problem, no matter how difficult it is, whether temporal or above all, spiritual, in the personal life of each one of us, of our families, of the families of the world, or of the religious communities, or even of the life of peoples and nations that cannot be solved by the Rosary. There is no problem I tell you, no matter how difficult it is, that we cannot resolve by the prayer of the Holy Rosary.[66]

Since our prayers and sacrifices build up the treasury of graces for souls, any progress we make in the pursuit of purity will benefit those around us. We can multiply this effect by embracing the sacrament of reconciliation and asking for the graces needed to let go of any stubborn attachments—to people, media, fashions, language, or behavior—that may be holding us back.

Tread very gently in the area of purity, praying for wisdom and making changes, slowly. It's best to set an example that is joyful, peace-loving, and kind. Husbands can be placed under the patronage of St. Joseph, the most chaste spouse of the Blessed Virgin Mary; he is very powerful and will gladly become a spiritual father and protector for your whole family. Remember that St. Peter said, "Above all, maintain constant love for one another, for love covers a multitude of sins" (1 Peter 4:8, NRSV).

Tiny, hidden sacrifices can go a long way, too. Denying ourselves little pleasures, like bigger servings of food, long showers, or that extra five minutes of sleep, can bring real vigor to our spiritual resolutions and pave the way for leaps of progress in the spiritual life. Likewise, resisting short-temperedness and holding back uncharitable comments are terrific ways to let go of our own pettiness and grow in the theological virtue of love.

And of course, it is most beneficial for our souls and the souls of the whole world when we prepare ourselves to receive, with holy reverence, our most merciful Jesus in the Holy Eucharist. To offer our reception of Holy Communion for an increase of purity in the world is to offer the infinite value of the Lord's own pure being, through which our spiritual redemption is made possible.

Chapter Nine

ALL THINGS NEW

Taking Stock and Moving Forward

And he who sat upon the throne said, "Behold, I make all
things new."

—Revelation 21:5

Growing up is a lifelong process. I like to think of it as growing right up
into God's presence, since each step we take toward his love leads us to
heaven. If we stay humble and curious about the ways of God, our lives
continue to be adventures full of opportunities to soak up graces and
become more radiant with each passing year. Each phase of our lives
prepares us for the next, as God builds his kingdom, brick by brick,
through our small acts of love.

Clearing the Way for the Next Phase of Your Life

Teach us to number our days
that we may get a heart of wisdom.

—Psalm 90:12

Before we look to the future, as maturing women, it can be helpful to
reflect on what has already been. Prayerfully looking back on our lives
and placing them in the context of God's will lays the foundation for
moving forward with courage and enthusiasm; as we reflect, patterns
may emerge that show us the outlines of God's handiwork. All along
the way, we have used the incomparable gift of our free will to make
choices, and God has stepped in, time and again, to bring blessings

out of our mistakes and help our good works bear fruit.

Of course, it's important to consider our personal histories with gentleness, to show compassion to ourselves and our families, to the people who have loved us and to those who have wounded us. It's how God looks at us—with eyes of love—and that love is everything. Without love, none of it makes sense. Without love, it is impossible to move on.

A wonderful woman at my parish, Bernadette, is a widow in her seventies. She cared for her sick husband for many years and has a son, John, who experienced severe head trauma in a car accident long ago. These days, he lives in a group home, where he is helped to live as independently as possible; but when the tragedy first occurred, the cataclysm of his misfortune was almost more than his mother could bear.

In the early days, when her son could neither walk nor speak, Bernadette spent many hours in tears, praying. She went through all the stages of grief, and at one point was outraged with God for not healing John, overwhelmed with the prospect of caring for her disabled son. One day, she knelt before the tabernacle in the sanctuary and poured out her anguished heart to Jesus. Even in the depths of fear and despair, she trusted him to answer.

Soon, his voice whispered tenderly in the quiet of her heart: *Bernadette, give the past to me; it belongs to me and I have redeemed it. Let go of the future. I have not yet entered into it and it belongs to me. I want you to be open to my love for you in the present moment, because I am always loving you like a river.* Bernadette says, "That's the way he wanted me to live the rest of my life." As peace descended into her heart, she knew she would be able to go on, to accept her crosses, and care for her son in a spirit of hope. She says that the twelve years she tended to him at home were a time of extraordinary graces and, amazingly, great joy.

Her life is a profile in courage. Because Bernadette is part of a weekly charismatic prayer group, she has surrounded herself with faith-filled friends who offer ongoing support. She receives Holy Communion most days and prays the rosary after Mass, so she is wrapped in the kind of confidence that only God can supply. To continue to receive such graces, she knows she must rest in God's holy will. "Everything is a gift," she says, "even when it's hard. God will help you with whatever you need."

When I review my own life, I vividly recall periods that seemed like a lot of senseless struggle at the time, but which God later used for his own sweet purposes. As a young actress, I experienced what a lot of naive and desperate "wannabes" discover, as they battle to make their way in the world of showbiz: moments of glory flecked into oceans of disappointment and failure.

I spent many years failing to build an acting career that would pay my bills and grant me some standing in the artistic community. There were independent and industrial films, television pilots, one-woman shows, off-off Broadway plays, improvisation troupes, and a little modeling along the way, but the seemingly endless slog of competing and searching for that one defining opportunity had left me wondering if I would ever find my place in the world. In 1992 I rededicated my life to Jesus Christ and everything began to change for the better.

Of course, there have been hard times along the way, but the blessings and healings have greatly outnumbered the difficulties, as my life is gradually being transformed in Christ. Whatever may come, I know that God, not me, will be the one who directs my steps and fills my days with purpose. He will be the one to bring beauty from ugliness, light from darkness, and joy from pain. His mercy will take my broken humanity and make something good come out of it.

Even though I chronically squander time on distractions, God hasn't wasted a moment of my life. I often say that all those years on stage and in front of cameras prepared me for my real vocation as a catechist. When I walk into a classroom, an auditorium, or a television studio, I feel at home, all the stage fright long since defeated through many professional acting experiences. And when my heart senses that an audience is opening its heart to my efforts to inspire and equip them with practical and spiritual insights and tools, I am overjoyed. I know I am home, that my broken life has been reassembled and resurrected for the true purpose that God planned for my life from the beginning.

I love—and try to live—this verse: "We know that in everything God works for good with those who love him, who are called according to his purpose" (Romans 8:28). Since God takes everything we give him and makes it into something beautiful, it makes a lot of sense to let go of anything we can't control and to give him our whole lives, past, present, and future.

Discerning God's Ongoing Call

The other day, a friend of mine was saying that Mother Teresa had beautiful eyes. It's true. If you look at any picture of her in which she is looking at another person, it is easy to believe that she truly saw Jesus Christ in every human face. Her eyes glow with the most tender affection. Since we are called to be the hands and voice and even the eyes of Christ in the world, it makes sense that her eyes would be so radiant with love; after all, Jesus had been looking through them for a long time. His presence in her was palpable.

But she was a saint, you're thinking. *What does that have to do with me?* I've felt that way, too, as if there existed a glass ceiling, spiritually speaking, and my prospects weren't anything special. In fact, I had pretty much reconciled myself to the thought that I would spend a

: in purgatory. I was just being realistic, I figured. But
·eresting exchange with Susan Tassone, the purgatory
...uioned in chapter six.[67]

Not long before I spoke with Susan, I had been reading St. Catherine of Siena's visions of purgatory[68] and made the happy mistake of remarking to Susan that I was actually looking forward to going to purgatory after death and getting cleaned up before coming into the presence of God. She was shocked and lovingly rebuked me, reminding me that God's grace is sufficient to make saints of every single one of us, and that it insults this free gift of grace to think otherwise.

So, let's stop to think about that statement. God's grace is sufficient to make saints of every single one of us. Note that Susan did not say that our own efforts or intentions are sufficient. If we respond to divine grace—not because of our own inherent sanctity, but out of humility and trust in God's mercy—we should not have to spend one single second in purgatory. Isn't that a game changer?

The thought that all the grace we need is at our disposal and we're still not saints makes me realize that God is all around us calling to us, offering us opportunities to draw closer and drink deeply of his love. We need to work at seeing those opportunities and taking them, even if it means sacrificing a little time in front of the TV or on our phones. It's essential to our growth in holiness that we commit ourselves to regular reception of the sacraments of Eucharist and reconciliation. Reading sacred Scripture feeds our souls with God's living presence and makes our thoughts and words shine with his radiant presence. Lives of the saints and other wholesome spiritual reading can help to restore our wounded imaginations, so battered by the commonplace obscenity of advertising and other media. When we fill our minds with thoughts that are good, true, and beautiful, we invite the Holy Spirit to transform us from the inside out. Remember that St. Paul advised us to feed our souls with beautiful thoughts and behaviors:

> Finally, brethren, whatever is true, whatever is honorable, whatever is just, whatever is pure, whatever is lovely, whatever is gracious, if there is any excellence, if there is anything worthy of praise, think about these things. What you have learned and received and heard and seen in me, do; and the God of peace will be with you. (Philippians 4:8–9)

Aside from the restoration of a holy imagination, which boosts our prayer lives and fuels our walk with God, inspirational reading and listening materials can help us to see our lives in the proper context. We are beloved daughters of God, heiresses to a great spiritual fortune. We are called to learn all we can about our inheritance, so that we can grasp it, live it, and share it. Jesus told his disciples, "Go into all the world and preach the gospel to the whole creation" (Mark 16:15), but first he carefully and lovingly taught them all that they needed to know to help bring others to faith. He didn't say, "Go with your gut. Make it up as you go along." He mentored them, slowly and patiently, over the course of three years, and then he sent the Holy Spirit to lead them even further.

It can be transformative just to admit that we don't know everything there is to know about our faith and make time for a little regular study. I love the *Catechism of the Catholic Church*, with its in-depth index and its many annotations, but many Catholics prefer the *YouCat* or the *Compendium*[69] for their question-and-answer formats. Tuning in to Catholic television and radio, DVDs or CDs[70] can be a great way to relax and build up your faith at the same time. Once you get started, you'll find that you hunger for material that nurtures your faith, and the Holy Spirit will help lead you to the next step in your spiritual and intellectual development.

Stoking the fire of our faith with ongoing learning enriches every part of our lives, enlivening spiritual values in the way we live. Acts of service, worship, daily praise, and the counting of blessings are manifestations of a sincere desire for intimacy with God. Mother Teresa famously said, "The fruit of silence is prayer, the fruit of prayer is faith, the fruit of faith is love, the fruit of love is service, the fruit of service is peace."[71] One step taken toward God leads to another and another. Every day is a new beginning, as we rise each morning to embrace the miracle of our existence. As each day is a gift, so our response to that gift is part of our conversation with God.

We are not all called to do great things, but we can all do little things with great love. Sound familiar? Paraphrased and misattributed with great regularity, this sentiment began with the diary of St. Thérèse of Lisieux, known as *Story of a Soul.* Mother Teresa was a lifelong devotee of the Little Way of St. Thérèse and expressed similar sentiments in her various talks and writings. But original sources aside, the sentiment is a powerful and appropriate one for every Christian to contemplate with seriousness.

I remember just after Christmas in 2004, a major earthquake occurred deep in the Indian Ocean, producing a devastating tsunami that killed almost a quarter of a million people in fourteen countries (principally Indonesia, Sri Lanka, India, and Thailand). Day after day, the images of devastation and death flooded the news, and reports of orphaned children being kidnapped and sold into sex slavery made the cataclysm infinitely more tragic to my maternal heart.

My own child safely at school and my husband at work, I was alone one day in prayer. On my knees in the living room, I was loudly sobbing, completely overwhelmed with a frantic desire to fly to Indonesia and help in the rescue efforts. To save even one little child would be everything to me. However, I have never been rich or powerfully connected, so this was an impossible hope. I felt my heart breaking from the torment of wanting to do more than was within my grasp, and it made me angry with God.

At the height of my prayer, I fell forward from the kneeling position onto all fours and cried to God aloud, "Why? Why have you put this desire in my heart if there is nothing I can do about it?" I roared at him, "Why have you made me so *useless*?" It is not possible to exaggerate the despair I felt in that moment. And then everything changed. Suddenly, it was as if God had placed his hand on me. My mind stilled. My tears stopped. Actual words formed in my heart unbidden. They were not my own.

You are where I have placed you.

In that moment, I looked around my small house and knew that I belonged there. I remembered the feelings of love that engulfed me the first time I crossed the threshold of the little cottage that would one day be my home. My work was here, in this little corner of creation, and—for that moment—nowhere else. My family's prayers and small donations to relief efforts were all we were asked to do. The rescuers had received their callings to serve on the ground at the disaster sites and would be supplied for by Providence. The ongoing drama did not cease to move me, but my peace had been restored. I would continue in the place ordained by God for me, loving and serving in my own tiny corner of the world.

True Radiance Revisited

Radiant beauty is something that comes from within. We can't buy it or wear it. It is something that emerges through a spirit of humble reliance on God. We may want liberation from the false ideals of our culture, but it's an ongoing struggle to avoid getting sucked back into a societal rut than runs deep and affects just about everyone around us. Because the messaging is so pervasive, it's all too easy to be caught up in an image of ourselves that is false and hurtful.

It makes me angry at the mass media when I notice women suffering over their looks, because I know exactly how they feel. No matter what we look like, there is always someone to take us down a peg. I've read that when Grace Kelly was starring in Hollywood films, her costume designers felt it necessary to create the illusion that her small fanny was rounder than it actually was. The 1960s fashion icon Twiggy, one of the most adored women of her generation, confesses that, as a young model, she stuffed her bra.[72] And apparently, one of the most photographed women in the world, Cindy Crawford, has said, "Even I don't wake up looking like Cindy Crawford."[73]

I have to shake my head! Some of the most gorgeous, successful women in the world have felt inadequate! We need to strip all our assumptions away and try to look at ourselves through God's eyes. To understand our holy, God-given feminine beauty, we must see ourselves through eyes of faith in the context of heaven, our true home. Here are some possible ways to think about the way God sees our true beauty.

Sometimes, when I'm singing in church, I notice the imperfections of all the human voices lifted in praise and worship and wonder what God hears when we sing. He can see the truth of our souls, so he must be able to hear the truth of our song. I have often wondered if our voices rise up with our prayers to heaven, transformed according to the depth of our love. I imagine the holiest and most humble among us bring the exceptional beauty of their souls to the resulting heavenly melody, while the rest of us add our simple, less-developed notes. In this daydream, all of our voices are greatly improved as they echo through the halls of heaven, because they are an expression of the goodness of our hearts, amplified through the intercession of the heavenly host.

Here's another way to think about our beauty in God's eyes. In J.R.R. Tolkien's short story, "Leaf by Niggle,"[74] an ordinary man with no great artistic talent, works away in his little shed, day after day, year after year, at a painting of a tree. Each leaf is carefully created with simple strokes of paint that any art critic would consider substandard, but Niggle never quits trying. At last, Niggle dies. On his soul's journey into the exquisite landscape of heaven, he is amazed to encounter his own tree, sprung into reality from the drab flatness of his earthly imaginings and standing gloriously beautiful, full of radiance and movement, on a grassy hill in paradise. His clumsy brush strokes have been lifted up by God and given life and loveliness beyond his wildest expectations, transformed into something authentic, exquisite, and eternal. His simple efforts have been allowed to bring beauty to the place of ultimate beauty.

I think of our bodies the same way. St. Paul reminds us, "'What no eye has seen, nor ear heard, / nor the heart of man conceived, / what God has prepared for those who love him,' / God has revealed to us through the Spirit" (1 Corinthians 2:9–10). If our bodies seem ordinary and imperfect to us, might that just be a reminder that our glorified bodies in heaven will surpass our wildest imaginings? Won't they be stronger, more lovely, more useful, and more meaningful? And won't God's idea of beauty make our cultural standards look like the shallow, laughable miscalculations we sense them to be? The sheer, agenda-driven inconsistency of human beauty ideals should be a wake-up call for us to question most of the prevailing fashions.

For instance, seventeenth-century artist Peter Paul Rubens presented the feminine ideal as a well-fed, sturdy woman. One can understand his wishful thinking, at a time of food shortages and high maternal death rates. Traditionally, the affluent Chinese wife of long ago had to be fat to prove her husband's prowess as a provider! At the rise of western feminism, empowered women were slapped down by an emaciated, immature ideal—think Twiggy—that sought to trap them in child-hood, where they couldn't threaten the very power structures they were preparing to climb! I hope you're laughing, because our lives are worth too much to spend them in anger over silliness that won't matter at all when we get to heaven.

In paradise I think we can expect that *our very selves* will blow our minds. If regret were possible in the divine kingdom, we might well say, "Well, shucks, I shouldn't have wasted my time trying to live up to such earthly nonsense. None of those ideas ever came close to what my body and soul really mean!"

The years of our maturity are not a time of dying beauty or a time for clinging to the past. The second half of our lives is bringing us, every moment, closer to heaven. Author Sarah Christmyer puts it this way:

> God never changes, even if you do, even if your situation does. He is the same God who had a plan when you were born and he had a plan as you were entering adulthood. He has a plan for you now, and it involves being a woman and being created for a special purpose. That purpose is not the same for everyone, but he's the same and he's keeping you in existence for a reason.

Sarah goes on to explain that our gift of receptivity is key at every stage of life:

> We need to listen to the Word of God: to spend time in silence, read our Bibles, pray and ask God to speak to our hearts. So

often, we just talk to him in prayer when what is needed is to listen for the voice of the Holy Spirit. Then, we must receive his word and act on what we hear. We may not understand or even like it, but we can throw ourselves on him for help, ask him to do in us as he wills.

The second half of life is a time of building on the past, growing in virtue, and deepening our connection with God, the source and summit of all beauty. Our beauty is not fading; it's getting more powerful. It's having more impact. It's becoming what it was meant to be from the beginning.

If only our eyes could see and our ears could hear what God has in store for those who love him! If we knew how beautiful our voices were, lifted in prayer and song; if we knew how beautiful God's plans were for our bodies and souls; if we knew the deeper meaning of every moment of our lives, we would treasure ourselves as the hints of heaven that we truly are.

A little reverence for ourselves is not amiss. We are made in God's image and likeness. We are temples of the Holy Spirit, a unity of meaningful body and eternal soul, to someday be cleansed and glorified and transformed into the truest expression of ourselves *for all eternity*. We really need to stop letting anybody tell us whether we are beautiful or not. God has already settled the matter. We are.

Your Feminine Gifts

Cooper O'Boyle, Donna-Marie. *Rooted in Love: Our Calling as Catholic Women.* Notre Dame, Ind.: Ave Maria, 2012.

Kineke, Genevieve. *The Authentic Catholic Woman.* Cincinnati: Servant, 2006.

Gohn, Pat. *Blessed, Beautiful, and Bodacious: Celebrating the Gift of Catholic Womanhood.* Notre Dame, Ind.: Ave Maria, 2013.

Pope John Paul II. *On the Dignity and Vocation of Women: Mulieris Dignitatem.*

Von Hildebrand, Alice. *The Privilege of Being a Woman.* Washington, D.C.: The Catholic University of America Press, 2005.

Zeno, Katrina J. *Discovering the Feminine Genius: Every Woman's Journey.* Boston: Pauline, 2010.

The Theology of the Body

Evert, Jason and Crystalina. *Theology of His Body/Theology of Her Body.* West Chester, Penn.: Ascension, 2009. (For teens, but excellent.)

Stimpson, Emily. *These Beautiful Bones: An Everyday Theology of the Body.* Steubenville, Ohio: Emmaus Road, 2013.

West, Christopher. *Theology of the Body for Beginners: A Basic Introduction to Pope John Paul II's Sexual Revolution,* revised edition. West Chester, Penn.: Ascension, 2009.

The Spiritual Life

Cooper O'Boyle, Donna-Marie. *A Catholic Woman's Book of Prayers.* Huntington, Ind.: Our Sunday Visitor, 2010.

De Montfort, St. Louis Marie. *The Secret of Mary.* Bay Shore, N.Y.: Montfort, 1994.

Heimann, Jean M. *Seven Saints for Seven Virtues.* Cincinnati: Servant, 2014.

Hendey, Lisa M. *The Grace of Yes: Eight Virtues for Generous Living.* Huntington, Ind.: Ave Maria, 2014.

Kreeft, Peter. *Prayer for Beginners.* San Francisco: Ignatius, 2000.

Scanlon, Michael, T.O.R., with James Manney. *What Does God Want? A Practical Guide to Making Decisions.* Huntington, Ind.: Our Sunday Visitor, 1994.

Sheen, Fulton J. *Life Is Worth Living.* San Francisco: Ignatius, 1999.

Spitzer, S.J., Fr. Robert. *Five Pillars of the Spiritual Life: A Practical Guide to Prayer for Active People.* San Francisco: Ignatius, 2008.

Tassone, Susan. *Day by Day for the Holy Souls in Purgatory: 365 Reflections.* Huntington, Ind.: Our Sunday Visitor, 2014.

———. *Praying with the Saints for the Holy Souls in Purgatory.* Huntington, Ind.: Our Sunday Visitor, 2009.

Thérèse of Lisieux. *Story of a Soul.* Washington, D.C.: ICS, 1996.

Authentic Beauty

O'Donohue, John. *Beauty, the Invisible Embrace: Rediscovering the True Sources of Compassion, Serenity, and Hope.* New York: Harper Perennial, 2005.

Saward, John. *The Beauty of Holiness and the Holiness of Beauty: Art, Sanctity & The Truth of Catholicism.* San Francisco: Ignatius, 1997.

Sullivan, Dr. Jem. *The Beauty of Faith: Using Christian Art to Spread the Good News.* Huntington, Ind.: Our Sunday Visitor, 2009.

For Healing

Popcak, Gregory K., Ph.D. *Broken Gods: Hope, Healing, and the Seven Longings of the Human Heart.* New York: Image, 2015. For more help, support, and information, contact Dr. Popcak's organization, Pastoral Solutions Institute. To make an appointment to speak with a counselor, call 704-266-6461, or visit his website, www.Catholic Counselors.com.

CatholicTherapists.com (a national directory of Catholic therapists faithful to the teachings of the Catholic Church).

Notes

1. The Brothers Grimm, *Grimm's Fairy Tales; Snow White,* 1812. http://en.wikipedia.org/wiki/Snow_White.
2. *Compendium of Social Doctrine of the Church,* no. 144. http://www.vatican.va/roman_curia/pontifical_councils/justpeace/documents/rc_pc_justpeace_doc_20060526_compendio-dott-soc_en.html.
3. Taken from a CD with the same title, *A Feather on the Breath of God: Sequences and Hymns by Saint Hildegard of Bingen* (London: Hyperion UK, 1993).
4. St. Louis Marie de Montfort, *The Secret of Mary* (Bay Shore, N.Y.: Montfort, 2001), p.18.
5. Father Robert Barron, "Evangelizing Through Beauty": https://www.youtube.com/watch?v=bBMOwZFpZX0; emphasis added.
6. Dr. Jem Sullivan, *The Beauty of Faith: Using Christian Art to Spread the Good News* (Huntington, Ind.: Our Sunday Visitor, 2009) p. 86.
7. Hans Urs von Balthasar, *The Glory of the Lord: A Theological Aesthetics, Volume I: Seeing the Form* (San Francisco: Ignatius, 1982), p. 18.
8. Bruce Marshall, *The World, the Flesh, and Father Smith* (Kingsport: Kingsport, Inc. 1945), p. 108.
9. Donna-Marie Cooper O'Boyle, *The Kiss of Jesus: How Mother Teresa and the Saints Helped Me to Discover the Beauty of the Cross* (San Francisco: Ignatius, 2015), p. 121.
10. The books containing her visions can be found by searching her name online.
11. The original *Baltimore Catechism* is in the public domain and can be found online, free, at many sites including CatholiCity.com.
12. John O'Donohue, *Beauty: The Invisible Embrace: Rediscovering the True Sources of Compassion, Serenity, and Hope* (New York: HarperCollins, 2004), p. 13.
13. Only a priest is permitted and able to do the consecration at Mass or to hear confessions (which is why deacons cannot perform the anointing of the sick), but a deacon may perform marriages and baptisms. In emergencies, laypeople are also permitted to perform baptisms.

14. Eric Metaxas, "Science Increasingly Makes the Case For God," *Wall Street Journal Online* (December 25, 2014), http://www.wsj.com/articles/eric-metaxas-science-increasingly-makes-the-case-for-god-1419544568.
15. Emily Stimpson, *These Beautiful Bones: An Everyday Theology of the Body* (Steubenville, Ohio: Emmaus Road, 2013), p. 26.
16. *To Women,* Second Vatican Council Closing Speeches and Messages, EWTN (December 8, 1965), http://www.ewtn.com/library/papaldoc/p6closin.htm.
17. Pope John Paul II, *Mulieris Dignitatem: On the Dignity and Vocation of Women,* http://www.vatican.va/holy_father/john_paul_ii/apost_letters/documents/hf_jp-ii_apl_15081988_mulieris-dignitatem_en.html.
18. See Recommended Resources
19. St. Louis Marie de Montfort, *The Secret of Mary* (Bay Shore, N.Y.: Montfort, 2001), p. 19.
20. Encyclical of Pope John Paul II, *Evangelium Vitae: To the Bishops, Priests and Deacons, Men and Women Religious, Lay Faithful, and all People of Good Will on the Value and Inviolability of Human Life*: The Holy See, http://w2.vatican.va/content/john-paul-ii/en/encyclicals/documents/hf_jp-ii_enc_25031995_evangelium-vitae.html.
21. Pope John Paul II: "Letter to Women for Beijing Conference": http://www.ewtn.com/library/PAPALDOC/JP2WOM.htm.
22. "Letter to Women for Beijing Conference," 5.
23. William Wordsworth, "The Virgin," *The Collected Poems of William Wordsworth* (Wordsworth Poetry Library, 1998). http://www.poetryfoundation.org/poem/174832.
24. Dietrich von Hildebrand was a renowned Catholic philosopher, theologian, professor, and author greatly admired by recent popes and Catholic intellectuals. He fled his native Germany under threat of arrest for speaking out against Hitler's atrocities and eventually settled in New York.
25. Alice von Hildebrand, Ph.D., *The Privilege of Being a Woman* (Ann Arbor, Mich.: Sapientia, 2002).

26. "10 Warning Signs," New York Chapter Alzheimer's Association, http://www.alz.org/nyc/in_my_community_62213.asp?gclid=Cj0KE QiAwaqkBRDHx6rzxMqAobgBEiQAxJazJ-dw0zVfq1FqEBoMy-ratdBmojevDiGPSXhP_p0_wTiMaAtPd8P8HAQ.
27. Deane Alban, "20 Medications That Cause Memory Loss," Be Brain Fit, http://bebrainfit.com/lifestyle/drains/20-medications-that-can-cause-memory-loss/.
28. Kate Volkman Oakes, "Pharmacy School Offers Real-Life Lessons in Precision Medicine," UCSF, http://www.ucsf.edu/news/2013/11/110321/brave-new-world.
29. The National Gianna Center for Women's Health and Fertility, 15 E. 40th Street, Suite 101, New York, NY 10016.
30. Dr. David Perlmutter, M.D., *Grain Brain: The Surprising Truth About Wheat, Carbs, and Sugar: Your Brain's Silent Killers* (New York: Little, Brown, 2013).
31. Dr. David Snowdon, *Aging with Grace: What the Nun Study Teaches Us About Leading Longer, Healthier, and More Meaningful Lives* (New York: Bantam, 2001), p. 79.
32. Snowdon, pp. 168–170.
33. Snowdon, p. 177.
34. Snowdon, pp. 192–193.
35. Snowdon, p. 202.
36. See Nicholas Carr, *The Shallows: What the Internet Is Doing to Our Brains* (New York/London: W.W. Norton & Company, 2010).
37. "Spiritual Communion Prayer": EWTN: https://www.ewtn.com/Devotionals/prayers/blsac4.htm.
38. Quoted with permission.
39. Lisa Mladinich, "Water into Wine": http://www.patheos.com/blogs/waterintowine/.
40. St. Thérèse of Lisieux, *Story of a Soul* (Washington, D.C.: ICS, 1997), p. 259.
41. *Story of a Soul*, p. 208.
42. From "A Wife," by Sir Thomas Overbury, circa 1613. See: an eudæmonist http://www.eudaemonist.com/biblion/overbury/wife.
43. Marcus Tullius Cicero, "Treatises on Friendship and Old Age": Project Gutenberg, http://www.gutenberg.org/files/2808/2808-h/2808-h.htm.

44. Lisa M. Hendey, *The Grace of Yes: Eight Virtues for Generous Living* (Notre Dame, Ind.: Ave Maria, 2014) p. 31.
45. Commentary on "The Book of Ruth" from *The New American Bible: Revised Edition* (Washington, D.C.: World Catholic, 2010), p. 260.
46. Luke 2:8–14, Psalm 33:6, Psalm 103:21, and many other Scriptures reference this heavenly "host."
47. St. Julian of Norwich, "Revelations of Divine Love," Christian Classics Ethereal Library, http://www.ccel.org/j/julian/revelations/.
48. *Story of a Soul,* p. 194.
49. For example, "The Dark Night," by St. John of the Cross: One True Name, http://onetrueame.com/StJohn.htm.
50. Pope Francis, *Lumen Fidei,* Holy See, http://w2.vatican.va/content/francesco/en/encyclicals/documents/papa-francesco_20130629_enciclica-lumen-fidei.html.
51. Zig Ziglar, "Zig on: Everybody Sells" www.ziglar.com (July 13, 2010), http://www.ziglar.com/newsletter/july-13-2010-edition-28.
52. *Story of a Soul,* p. 220, emphasis added.
53. *Story of a Soul,* p. 234.
54. Susan Davis, "Addicted to Your Smart Phone? Here's What to Do," WebMD, http://www.webmd.com/balance/guide/addicted-your-smartphone-what-to-do.
55. See Carr.
56. Heather Hatfield, "Power Down For Better Sleep," WebMD, http://www.webmd.com/sleep-disorders/features/power-down-better-sleep.
57. Bill Hendrick, "Internet Overuse May Cause Depression," WebMD, http://www.webmd.com/depression/news/20100802/internet-overuse-may-cause-depression.
58. Message of the Holy Father Benedict XVI for the 43rd World Communications Day, 7.
59. Kim Parker and Eileen Patten, "The Sandwich Generation: Rising Financial Burdens for Middle Aged Americans," Pew Research Center January 30, 2013), http://www.pewsocialtrends.org/2013/01/30/the-sandwich-generation/.
60. Fr. Robert Spitzer, S.J., *Pillars of the Spiritual Life: A Practical Guide to Prayer for Active People* (San Francisco: Ignatius, 2008).
61. *Story of a Soul,* p. 242.

62. Pope Benedict XVI, *The Joy of Knowing Christ: Meditations on the Gospels* (Frederick, Md.: The Word Among Us, 2009), p. 12, emphasis added.

63. Fulton J. Sheen, *Life Is Worth Living* (San Francisco: Ignatius, 1999) p. 255.

64. "Pornography Statistics," Covenant Eyes, http://www.covenanteyes. com/pornstats/.

65. John O'Donohue, *Beauty, the Invisible Embrace: Rediscovering the True Sources of Compassion, Serenity, and Hope* (New York: HarperCollins, 2004), p. 4.

66. "The Rosary," http://fatima.ageofmary.com/rosary/.

67. See Susan Tassone, *Day by Day for the Holy Souls in Purgatory: 365 Reflections* (Huntington, Ind.: Our Sunday Visitor, 2014).

68. St. Catherine of Siena, *Fire of Love! Understanding Purgatory* (Manchester, N.H.: Sophia Institute, 1996).

69. *Compendium of the Catechism of the Catholic Church*, Holy See http://www.vatican.va/archive/compendium_ccc/documents/ archive_2005_compendium-ccc_en.html.

70. See Recommended Resources for recommendations.

71. "Her Words," EWTN, https://www.ewtn.com/motherteresa/words. htm.

72. Jess Cartner-Morley, "Twiggy at 60: 'It's amazing I didn't go stark raving bonkers,'" *The Guardian* (September 19, 2009), http://www. theguardian.com/lifeandstyle/2009/sep/19/twiggy-at-60-interview.

73. David Keeps, "Get a Peek Inside Cindy Crawford's Home," *Redbook* (August 17, 2009), http://www.redbookmag.com/home/interviews/ a5192/cindy-crawford-interview/.

74. J.R.R. Tolkien, "Leaf by Niggle," Tolkien Gateway, http://tolkien-gateway.net/wiki/Leaf_by_Niggle.